THE NATIONAL INTEREST

AND THE

TEACHING OF ENGLISH

A Report on the Status of the Profession

Prepared by the Committee on National Interest

James R. Squire, *Chairman*

Harold B. Allen

George H. Henry

J. N. Hook

Albert H. Marckwardt

Richard A. Meade

Joseph Mersand

Eugene E. Slaughter

George Winchester Stone, Jr.

Ruth G. Strickland

THE NATIONAL COUNCIL OF TEACHERS OF ENGLISH
508 South Sixth Street   Champaign, Illinois

COMMITTEE ON PUBLICATIONS

Richard Corbin, Hunter College High School, New York
Muriel Crosby, Wilmington, Delaware, Public Schools
William S. Ward, University of Kentucky
James R. Squire, University of Illinois, Chairman

Enid Olson, Publications Associate, NCTE

Copyright 1961
The National Council of Teachers of English

WHEREAS the Golden Anniversary White House Conference on Children and Youth this year recommended greater emphasis on humanistic studies in education; and

WHEREAS the Conference recommended the establishment of a National Humanities Foundation to offer needed support and encouragement of the humanities on a national scale; and

WHEREAS English is a humanistic study most basic and most often taken by students, and the teacher of English is thus the representative of the humanities in the elementary and secondary schools; be it

RESOLVED that the National Council of Teachers of English

1. Support all national efforts to obtain support for the teaching of English and the other humanities on a national scale; and

2. Direct its Executive Committee to inform the nation's leaders in government, business, and education of the Council's mounting concern over the neglect of English and the other humanities in current educational efforts; and furthermore

3. Direct its Executive Committee to inform the Congress of the United States and the United States Office of Education of the compelling need for an extension of the National Defense Education Act of 1958 to include English and the humanities as a vital first step toward improving instruction in English and of stimulating program development in this important area.

—Resolution adopted at the Golden Anniversary Meeting of the National Council of Teachers of English

November 24, 1960

READERS OF THE MANUSCRIPT WHO OFFERED MANY HELPFUL SUGGESTIONS WERE:

For the American Council of Learned Societies

    Albert H. Marckwardt, *University of Michigan*

For the American Council on Education

    Raymond F. Howes, *Staff Associate, American Council on Education*

For the College English Association

    John Hicks, *University of South Florida*
    Donald Lloyd, *Wayne State University*
    Donald A. Sears, *Upsala College*

For the American Studies Association

    Joseph Schiffman, *Dickinson College*

For the Modern Language Association of America

    George Winchester Stone, Jr., *New York University*

For the National Council of Teachers of English

    Robert A. Bennett, *Minneapolis Public Schools*
    Dwight L. Burton, *Florida State University*
    G. Robert Carlsen, *State University of Iowa*
    John J. DeBoer, *University of Illinois*
    Alfred H. Grommon, *Stanford University*
    Brice Harris, *The Pennsylvania State University*
    Lou L. LaBrant, *Dillard University*
    Richard Lander, *Shoreline High School, Seattle, Washington*
    Glenn Leggett, *University of Washington*
    James J. Lynch, *University of California, Berkeley*
    Harold C. Martin, *Harvard University*
    Henry C. Meckel, *San Jose State College*
    James E. Miller, Jr., *University of Nebraska*
    Dora V. Smith, *University of Minnesota*
    Erwin R. Steinberg, *Carnegie Institute of Technology*
    Donald R. Tuttle, *Fenn College*

Contents

PART I
What Has to Be Done about the National Need to Improve the Teaching of English...... 1

PART II
The National Problem.....................13

PART III
The Status of English Teaching Today........31

THE NEED FOR MORE TEACHERS OF ENGLISH

THE NEED FOR BETTER TEACHERS OF ENGLISH

    A Standard of Preparation to Teach English

    State Certification Regulations for Teaching English

    The Preparation of the Elementary Teacher in English

    The English Language Preparation of Secondary Teachers of English

    The Preparation in Literature of Secondary Teachers of English

THE NEED FOR BETTER TEACHING CONDITIONS

    The Conditions under Which English Is Taught

    The Inadequacy of School Library and Book Resources

    The Cost of Remedial Instruction at the College Level

    High Schools That Produce Superior English Students

THE NEED FOR BETTER AND MORE BASIC RESEARCH IN ENGLISH

A Final Word..............................136

Index 137

PART I

What Has to Be Done about the National Need to Improve the Teaching of English

- Projects to Assist in Focusing the Teaching of English upon the Study of Language, Literature, and Composition
- Projects to Assist in Educating Teachers to the Developmental and Sequential Nature of English Studies and to Encourage Articulation throughout the School Years
- Projects to Improve Present Preparatory Programs for Teachers of English
- Projects to Improve the Preparation of Practicing Teachers
- Provisions to Obtain Services and Supplies for Teachers of English
- Projects to Assist in Encouraging Research and Scholarship
- Projects to Assist in Recruiting More Teachers of English

I
What Has to Be Done about the National Need to Improve the Teaching of English

If the teaching of English is to be improved throughout the country, bold and immediate action must be undertaken on a national scale. This report on the status of English teaching indicates that assistance is urgently needed to achieve seven important goals:

To focus instruction in English upon the study of language, literature, and composition

To educate teachers of English to the developmental and sequential nature of the study and to institute a national program for encouraging articulation of English studies throughout the school years

To improve present preparatory programs for teachers of English

To improve the preparation of practicing teachers of English

To improve the services and supplies available to teachers of English

To encourage significant research about the teaching of English

To recruit and prepare more teachers of English

All of these items hinge upon each other. Encouragement of them will alone make for a dynamic profession and ultimately bring about the results of excellence which the national interest requires. Most of them involve too much expenditure to be borne by a single foundation or a single professional group. To undertake many of them on an independent basis locally is to waste money and energy and to avoid the participation of the best minds and methods nationally. The basic problems of improving the preparation of teachers and of articulating the study at all levels of education are so important and so large that they can be undertaken only by a nationally supported program. Some projects to help achieve these purposes are recommended for attention:

A. *Projects to Assist in Focusing the Teaching of English upon the Study of Language, Literature, and Composition*

Pages 26-27, 48-86*

1. *Developing a widespread national institute program for elementary and secondary teachers.* A highly developed program of institutes, each carrying proper academic credit, could provide the foundation for training elementary teachers and secondary teachers of English in the essential content and methods of English. Such a program should involve college teachers now in service and those now preparing teachers.

2. *Encouraging teams of college scholars to work with teachers in local schools.* Among the more promising ways of bringing together university scholarship and secondary school teaching are programs which provide for teams of selected college specialists in English language, literature, composition, and the teaching of English to meet continuously over a period of time with high school teachers for the purpose of improving the teachers' knowledge and skill. Financial assistance is needed to enable colleges and schools to release teachers for such team programs. In a major school system one specialist could presumably direct several such programs simultaneously (for instance, working with one group on Monday through the year, another on Tuesday, and so on). But teachers in such a program need some time off from teaching and hence need assurance of no loss in compensation. Such programs would also be feasible for communities within travel distance of a college or university.

3. *Encouraging follow-up seminars throughout a school year.* Summer institutes followed by regular seminar meetings during a school year prove especially effective in assisting teachers to apply new knowledge in the classroom. Language, composition, and literature may be studied intensively during the summer; ways of applying the newly acquired knowledge in the classroom may be considered during evening seminars throughout the year. Since participating teachers in these seminars are facing students throughout the day, the seminar sessions prove especially realistic and practical.

4. *Recommending that English examinations given prospective supervisors or teachers be both comprehensive and accurate.* English consists primarily of the study of literature, language, and composition. Any examination purporting to test knowledge of English should include some assessment of background in these three areas. Any test should be accurate, thorough, and consistent with modern scholarship.

5. *Familiarizing administrators, school boards, and parents concerning the content of English.* Much confusion in English results from

---

*Refer to pages listed in the margin for a discussion of the need.

demands made on teaching time by community and administrative pressures. An intensive educational campaign needs to be waged throughout the country to inform professional and lay leaders of the significance of the content of English and of the need to permit the teacher of English to focus on his central responsibilities.

B. *Projects to Assist in Educating Teachers to the Developmental and Sequential Nature of English Studies and to Encourage Articulation throughout the School Years*

Pages 27-28

1. *Encouraging study of the problems of articulation in institutes, conferences, and special projects.* Special provision needs to be made for a consideration of the problems of sequence and continuity in all institutes, conferences, and curricular projects concerned with the teaching of English. The complexity of all content must be studied in relation to the maturity of the learners and to their differing backgrounds, needs, and abilities. Specialists in the teaching of English at the elementary, secondary, and college levels must be involved. Even in programs intended for teachers at a particular grade level, ways must be found to relate immediate concerns over content and method to a consideration of the over-all English program.

Pages 28-30

2. *Increasing coordination and supervisory services in state and local school districts.* To provide the needed leadership in program development and in-service education, specialists in the teaching of English are needed on the staff of every state department of education. Such supervisors should be persons especially prepared by education and experience to promote sound articulation of programs in English from the kindergarten through the high school, as well as articulation between the high school and the college. States unable to employ permanent supervisors might arrange to obtain the temporary services of a college or university faculty member to assist on a special project.

Pages 27-28

3. *Establishing regional centers for study and demonstration.* Development of a series of key regional centers for study and demonstration of sequential, articulated programs in English for a heterogeneous student population would effectively dramatize to the nation the need for improving English instruction at all grade levels. With financial assistance to make possible the needed facilities and staff, selected universities and state departments of education could establish programs to serve as touchstones by which all their school programs might measure themselves. Provision could be made at such centers for demonstration of sound programs, for experimentation with new methods and materials,

for demonstration to teachers and administrators, for the development of new curriculum materials. Especially important would be provision that the student populations be heterogeneous, like those faced in average American communities. Such centers could provide leadership in higher education, no less than in elementary and secondary education.

C. *Projects to Improve Present Preparatory Programs for Teachers of English*

Pages 49, 61, 75

1. *Supporting special conferences of college and university personnel concerned with the education of teachers of English.* Special conferences of selected college and university personnel (department heads; language, literature, and composition specialists; English education specialists; chairmen of freshman composition) could be called to consider the major problems which are highlighted in this report, with the specific purpose of revising and improving preparatory programs at their own and other institutions.

2. *Establishing pilot programs in teacher education.* Assistance in program development at teacher training institutions may have far reaching results, especially when the new programs are of a type to be continued ultimately by institutions without outside help. Special assistance may be provided to assist institutions to meet the costs of initial planning, of involving outside experts, and of evaluating results.

Pages 28-29

3. *Distributing information on experimental or pilot programs which are attempted.* Where new programs to educate teachers are introduced, information about the successes and failures must be disseminated. Outside observers from the United States Office of Education, from state departments of education, or from national foundations—whichever are appropriate—should review programs objectively and report with reasonable speed to key members of the profession. Provision should be made in all new programs for careful evaluation and reporting.

4. *Providing for outside observers to attend conferences on teacher education programs.* Where summer institutes or experimental programs are initiated by the United States Office of Education or other national agencies, selected educational leaders should be invited to attend. For example, were staff members from a dozen universities to plan coordinated summer institutes for teachers of English, a few state superintendents might be invited to attend. Were special summer conferences held on selected university campuses throughout the land, department heads from nonparticipating colleges in each region might be encouraged to attend as visitors. Participation of this kind not only facilitates com-

munication on new projects but also encourages development of companion programs.

5. *Supporting summer institutes for the graduates of small colleges.* Graduates of small colleges not offering much preparation in linguistics, composition, literature, the psychology of learning English, or other specialized work should be brought together in summer institutes for a concentrated course before they undertake their regular teaching in September.

D. Projects to Improve the Preparation of Practicing Teachers

Pages 86-87

1. *Establishing special scholarships or loans.* Thousands of teachers now teaching English but lacking adequate background need financial assistance if they are to educate themselves to meet reasonable standards. Many persons unable to meet the minimum legal standards for teaching English in their states, but who nevertheless are teaching on emergency certificates, need to return to college for special training. A program of summer scholarships or loans (perhaps loans forgivable up to fifty per cent after five years of subsequent service in teaching) will encourage such self-improvement. Legislation similar to S3481 (introduced in the 1960 session of the Senate by Sen. Ralph Yarborough and others) or HR12140 (introduced by Rep. Frank Kowalski) is urgently needed. Some teachers of English are so deficient in preparation that they need to take many courses; consequently, legislation needs to provide for scholarships or loans extended over several summers so that sequential work in related courses may be planned under the supervision of an institution of higher education.

Pages 74-75

2. *Expanding summer and establishing year-long institute offerings in English and the humanities.* Increased opportunities for attending summer institutes in English will encourage self-education in the humanities. Programs similar to those sponsored in 1960 on a small scale by the American Council of Learned Societies need to be expanded. Especially needed in English are institutes which provide experienced teachers with an opportunity to review recent scholarship in language, composition, literature, the psychology of learning, and developments in the teaching of English at the elementary and secondary levels.

Pages 35-36

3. *Encouraging more graduate level programs and summer and/or year-long institutes for English teachers without college English majors.* Many persons teaching English without an English major lack the necessary course prerequisites for admission to graduate level classes in English. Because some local boards of education consider only graduate

credit in awarding salary increments, many non-majors who teach English are discouraged from taking additional work in their subject. Ways need to be found to encourage such teachers to study English, possibly through providing special institutes or in-service courses which will ultimately prepare them for regular graduate work. State and local leaders can try to persuade local boards to accept upper-division undergraduate studies in English in awarding salary increments to non-major teachers in the secondary schools or to elementary teachers. Such courses will bring the non-major somewhat closer to the major in his preparation to teach English.

Pages 28, 74-75

4. *Supporting large-scale experimental projects (perhaps on a matching fund basis) involving a whole school system, or several comparable school systems, especially on the application of linguistic materials to the teaching of English.* For example, such projects could provide cooperating linguistic and educational experts working as a team. These scholars could prepare materials and direct controlled experiments in applying linguistic knowledge and methods throughout the English curriculum over a period of several years. Cooperating teachers would need in-service training or pre-training. Such projects might assess the effectiveness of the linguistic approach by measuring improvement in language facility. Similar projects could be sponsored in composition and literature.

5. *Encouraging study of experimental programs already in operation.* Greater provision needs to be made for studying at a national level the experiments in English and the humanities which are already underway in various places. Careful evaluation of such programs by impartial observers and dissemination of results might prove especially fruitful. Too often, inadequate provisions are made for evaluating experimental projects, and the results (both negative and affirmative) remain relatively unknown.

Pages 36-37

6. *Promoting summer conferences for college instructors.* Many college instructors, especially those in junior colleges, small liberal arts colleges, and technical schools, need continual opportunity to renew and advance their study of English and the teaching of English. Special conferences, possibly scheduled for a limited period of three or four weeks after the termination of regular summer sessions, can provide many of the needed refresher courses. Such conferences should probably concentrate on recent developments in scholarship.

Pages 19, 23-24

7. *Promoting special conferences on critical problems facing teachers of English such as on the teaching of English in culturally depressed communities.* Assistance, such as special conferences, must be provided for

teachers, administrators, supervisors, psychologists, and social workers confronting new problems resulting from changes in our society. For example, one of the pressing problems facing urban schools is the changing nature of the school population resulting from population mobility. Because the cultural background of children profoundly influences their language development, teachers in many areas confront new or unfamiliar problems in helping the children acquire basic language facility. Special conferences could be called to study such pressing problems and to recommend specially designed programs in English for these areas.

8. *Encouraging conferences to develop ways and means of improving English teaching at all schools, independent as well as public.* The need for improving the quality of education extends to all of the nation's schools and colleges, whether private or public. Ways need to be found to improve the training and background of English teachers in independent schools and colleges as well as of those in public schools and colleges. Special conferences might be needed to assure that all programs for improvement are educationally comprehensive.

E. Provisions to Obtain Services and Supplies for Teachers of English

1. *Assisting in the establishment of regional centers for English instruction.* Development of regional centers for study and demonstration of English instruction could be encouraged were special financial assistance available. To serve a national purpose, such centers would necessarily have to be developed cooperatively by selected school districts, key universities, and state departments of education. Such centers could prepare and distribute sample teaching aids, provide consultant help for teachers, and supplement services available in local school districts.

2. *Providing special financial inducements to encourage advanced study by English teachers with demonstrated leadership potential.* A program of scholarships or grants could encourage outstanding teachers to prepare themselves for exercising leadership in local school districts in improving the English curriculum. Colleges and universities could be encouraged to offer doctoral programs in the teaching of English. The present John Hay Whitney scholarship program is already providing a limited number of teachers with the opportunity to live for a year in a cultural climate for the purpose of restimulating their imaginations and their minds. More programs of this type are needed.

3. *Advising school architects and school administrators concerning the special building requirements needed for English teaching.* Composition, literature, and language are taught more effectively in rooms which

permit the storage of books and papers, as well as the use of recordings, tape recorders, and other audio-visual aids. Teachers and students require conference space and work space. Too many architects plan classrooms without considering how the rooms will be used. At the national and state levels, the special room needs of English teaching should be made known to school architects, perhaps by presentation of sample plans. Similar suggestions should be made to assure adequate, well-planned school libraries.

Pages 134-135

4. *Experimenting with using electronic and audio-visual aids in teaching English.* Provisions in Title VII of the National Defense Education Act of 1958 encourage experimentation in use of the media but *not* specifically in using the media to teach subject matter. Teachers of English need to find whether there are sound ways to teach English through the use of teaching machines, tape recordings, educational television, and other such devices and media. Great progress in using these aids in teaching English and the humanities is more likely to occur if emphasis in research can be placed on the teaching of English through these media, rather than on the media alone. Assistance in installing language laboratories, educational television equipment, listening rooms, and other special aids in the nation's schools and colleges would encourage the experimentation likely to lead to the successful exploitation of electronic and audio-visual aids in the teaching of English.

Pages 100-104

5. *Assisting in developing adequate library facilities.* Few objects are as necessary to education as adequate books. Increased library resources are needed at elementary, secondary, and college levels. A national program to ensure development of adequate library facilities and books for all American youth, possibly supplemented by an expansion of state library services to local school districts, would strengthen instruction in every area and at every instructional level. Special financial assistance (perhaps on a matching fund basis) may be needed to develop needed facilities in impoverished school districts.

F. Projects to Assist in Encouraging Research and Scholarship

Pages 133-135

1. *Supporting research basic to the teaching of English.* Funds are needed to support and encourage research related to many basic problems in English. For example, vitally needed is a study of classroom applications of recent research in language by psychologists, linguists, and specialists in methodology.

Pages 89-100

2. *Supporting research related to teaching conditions and to the utilization of the teacher's time.* Impartial and controlled studies are

10

needed now to assess the effects on student learning of new proposals for utilizing the teacher's time or for modifying teaching loads, school schedules, e.g., the effects of team teaching, large group lecturing, use of lay readers, inter-age grouping, schedule modification, etc. Such studies should be both initiated and encouraged by the United States Office of Education. Among the important problems needing deeper investigation are the relationship between the size of the class and student learning; the nature of the development of language abilities in children and youth; the factors and conditions which influence the selection of textbooks used in the schools.

G. Projects to Assist in Recruiting More Teachers of English

Page 33

1. *Offering special inducements to liberal arts graduates.* Recent experimentation in many colleges and universities has demonstrated the success of fifth-year programs of teacher preparation for liberal arts graduates who have little or no course work in professional education. Recruitment may be encouraged by offering such graduates special financial inducements or by underwriting some of the costs of expensive, experimental teaching internship programs, e.g., "earn-while-you-learn" programs in which graduates engage in part time paid teaching along with part time graduate studies under the close supervision of specialists

Pages 21-22, 38

at a teacher training institution. Especially needed are fellowships or stipends to assist highly qualified liberal arts graduates to undertake graduate studies in preparation for teaching English. States and institutions will interest more liberal arts graduates in entering elementary or secondary teaching by permitting qualified applicants to substitute valid experience or special examinations for some of the required courses. The current inflexibility of many credential regulations often prevents a mature student from embarking on a teacher training program. Such substitution should be encouraged, however, only when a candidate provides substantial proof of his competence in the necessary phases of English or education.

Page 37

2. *Expanding scholarship and loan programs for students planning to teach English and the humanities.* An increase in presently available scholarships and loans will encourage students of English and the humanities to prepare to teach. Title II of the National Defense Education Act of 1958 now offers a priority in obtaining loan funds to students in science, mathematics, and the foreign languages. This discriminating priority system should be extended to include students in English and the humanities.

Pages 133-135

3. *Distributing more comprehensive career information on the demand for English specialists.* Some national agency or institution should provide accurate, comprehensive information on the nation's need for specialists in English and the humanities with the aim of recruiting future teachers in the nation's colleges. Such a campaign will require financial support. At present, information reaches college and high school counselors only sporadically. A well-planned, long-range program of research, fact finding, and reporting should be conducted by a division of the United States Office of Education or some similar agency.

Page 65

4. *Developing a "Visiting Scholar Program" directed at enlisting undergraduate liberal arts students in teaching and interesting high school teachers in advanced study.* Many undergraduates in liberal arts colleges and junior colleges throughout the country could be attracted to graduate study in English and ultimately to teaching in schools and colleges if an intensive program of recruitment were undertaken by college specialists. The effective Visiting Scholar Program of the American Mathematics Association could well serve as a model. A similar program might be introduced to acquaint high school teachers with developments in linguistics and literature as well as the opportunities for advanced study.

Page 132

5. *Offering special summer programs in the humanities for the academically talented in high school.* Only if a reasonable percentage of able high school students continue study of English and the humanities in college will these fields be assured of a continuing supply of competent teachers for tomorrow's classrooms. Those high school students who demonstrate high interest and proficiency in English and in related fields need special encouragement. A series of national summer programs in the humanities, especially designed for high school students, would do much to encourage interest. Programs might promote the study and discussion of great works of literature under the supervision of distinguished college teachers, or they might provide for study of the English language through a series of especially designed lectures and study groups.

PART II

The National Problem

- The teaching of English plays a vital role in preserving human values in our technological society.
- Our democratic institutions depend upon intelligent, informed communication.
- Competence in using English is essential in every subject.
- English is taught more extensively to more pupils than is any other subject.
- The demand for English teachers has increased faster than the number adequately trained.
- The old and essential obligations of the English teacher have not changed, but new obligations make his task increasingly difficult.
- English and its teachers should focus on the study of language, literature, and composition.
- Poorly prepared teachers of English have created a serious national problem.
- Probably the greatest single weakness is the lack of articulation in the teaching of English.
- National concern about the deficiencies of English instruction has become almost commonplace.
- Coordinated national and state efforts are needed to improve the teaching of English.

II

The National Problem

In this country more pupils spend more time more continuously throughout their entire schooling on the subject of English than on any other subject. Competence in English is almost universally acknowledged as basic to quality in education. Two of the three R's are included in the subject. Yet the teaching of English in this country is far less effective than it should be. Too many students are struggling to learn English under gravely inferior conditions—in crowded classrooms with inadequate books; from teachers ill-prepared and insufficiently helped; in schools unable to attract and to retain teachers with the vision and experience to develop strong English programs; sometimes with skills, especially in reading and writing, that have been insufficiently developed at earlier educational levels.

This report on the conditions under which English is at present taught in this country suggests the vigorous action needed to improve the teaching. Section I outlined a series of recommendations. This section explains why the need is national. Section III presents a comprehensive picture of the status of English teaching today. The reasons for a national effort to improve the teaching of English are both compelling and urgent.

1. *The teaching of English plays a vital role in preserving human values in our technological society.* Since most elementary and secondary school pupils in the United States meet a humanistic study only by their continuous and sequential study of English, the English teacher becomes for them *the* representative of the humanities. The importance of English—the language and its literature—lies in its hold upon the intellect and the emotions of man. The processes of becoming articulate and literate are central to man's attainment of full human dignity; literature helps man to understand his own nature and the nature of fellow human beings; literature reveals and clarifies reality, affording illumination—rugged, intellectually demanding and inspiring—of the ideas and experiences of man. The cultivation of literature not only gives man an access to the ideas and values of his culture and a consequent desire

The humanistic values of English

to cherish and improve it but also stimulates his growth in understanding, sensitivity, and compassion. To be able to speak and write clearly about this illumination and understanding is to be an articulate, mature participant in what is most essentially human. When the 1960 White House Conference on Youth, in two separate recommendations, calls for greater emphasis on the humanities in the school curriculum,[1] there is only one possible answer: a revitalization and rededication in its role of preserving and transmitting the humanistic tradition.

The young who study our language and literature come into the best contact possible with the dreams, hopes, and aspirations, as well as with the roots of our culture. The rich texture of myth and folklore of lumbering, pioneering, and railroading stimulates the imagination and is a vehicle for the perpetual transmission of the American heritage. Only through the imagination do the complex natures of our various regions—Down East, the Old South, the prairie, the corn belt, and the mining town—become ingrained in our rising generations. Many of the books our youth read suggest the richness which we define as our heritage—*Our Town, Huckleberry Finn,* "The Devil and Daniel Webster," "The Death of the Hired Man," *Abe Lincoln in Illinois, The Scarlet Letter, Moby Dick.* These stories are founded upon an older and wider tradition, but one still ours—*David Copperfield,* "The Ancient Mariner," "The Deserted Village," "Elegy Written in a Country Church Yard," *Robinson Crusoe, Macbeth.* And this literature depends upon and blends with an even older tradition—the temptations of Faust, the mystic Bluebird, the penetrating humor of Don Quixote, the wanderings of Ulysses, the heroic figures of Greek and Roman myth, the just and overseeing God of the Bible. The base of the heritage is as broad as the humanistic tradition.

2. *Our democratic institutions depend upon intelligent, informed communication, which in turn depends upon the training of all persons to think critically and imaginatively, to express themselves clearly, and to read with understanding.* Man's ability to communicate information, feelings, and values distinguishes him as human. The success with which he leads his life depends upon his ability to conduct his personal affairs effectively with other people, to contribute sensibly to community life, and to share the experience of others—men of the past and of distant places, as well as of contemporaries. Every man's ability to achieve a satisfying personal life and to share in the responsibilities and opportunities of

The social value of English

---

[1]Recommendations 138 and 139 (Forums V, XI, and XII), *Conference Proceedings,* Golden Anniversary White House Conference on Children and Youth (Washington, D.C.: Government Printing Office, 1960), p. 333.

society depends upon his ability to read, write, and speak well his mother tongue.

Buffeted by the problems of our twentieth century democracy—complex organization, sudden technological changes, the passionate pressure of self-seeking groups, conflicting ideologies, uncertainty about the future, baffling international problems—modern man must cope with his work, make wise choices, and respond to the exacting demands of intelligent citizenship. His success will depend in no small measure not only on his ability to think, to read, and to express his ideas clearly, but also on his acquiring perspective by acquaintance with the best that has been known and thought in the past.

Young people living in the twentieth century are studying new attitudes toward space and time, new concepts about the nature of the universe—ideas which raise profound questions about the role of man in his world and about man's philosophical and spiritual views. Problems of this kind are becoming a major concern in the lives of many people and reveal a need for much reading and study about the role of man in this world.

In our world, too, where East meets West in almost daily encounter, when travelers and businessmen represent our culture and our values no less than do our statesmen and military personnel—in a world in which the profile of the "Ugly American" is all too vividly etched—it is important that Americans everywhere fully understand their heritage and see themselves not only as bearers of aid, technology, and materialism but also of ideas, of human dignity and freedom—ideas articulated with such vision by Jefferson, Lincoln, Emerson, Thoreau, and Whitman—ideas derived in the tradition of the French democrats and the Magna Carta, through the writings of Milton and Schiller and Sophocles, influenced by the philosophy of Locke and Dante and Aristotle. The encounter between the East and West need not be a clash of spiritual and material views but can result in a mutual exchange of spiritual and cultural values. If all Americans are to become ambassadors, all must educate themselves deeply in their own and the world's literature.

3. *Competence in using English is essential in every subject. Unless English is taught well, every subject suffers.* Because language is the vehicle for ideas, command of language is important in every subject. The task of educating students to use language is the special responsibility of the English teacher, but his success or failure ultimately affects instruction in all other subjects. "Without the ability to read accurately and to write clear, coherent prose, no engineer, scientist, architect, or

Learning depends on language

business executive can achieve distinction in his profession," states J. C. Warner, president of Carnegie Institute of Technology.

A recent survey of leaders in American business, government, law, and communications clearly reveals their firm belief in the paramount importance of English studies.[2] Typical of the comments is the reaction from W. W. Watson, chairman of the physics department, Yale University, who believes English to be "the most important subject in the entire course of study in the elementary and college preparatory years" or that of John F. Latimer, professor of classics and assistant dean of faculties, the George Washington University, who asserts, "We must learn that English is the mother and father of all disciplines for us and for all who speak English as a native tongue." English is a bedrock subject. Knowledge and skill in English are basic to the attainment of excellence, whether in regular schools and college programs, in graduate or professional study, or in professional service.

The extent to which advanced students are hampered by their inadequate command of English was recently summoned to attention in a national survey of graduate education in the United States.[3] In 1959 the American Bar Association devoted a special section of its annual meeting to considering the problem of language deficiency. A year earlier the Educational Policies Committee of the Association of Graduate Schools proposed a graduate entrance examination to include English composition.

The careless writing in American professional journals often impedes communication between writer and reader. (Compare, for example, the literary quality of the British medical journal, *Lancet*, with that of any comparable publication in this country.) A recent survey of leaders of the business world suggests that inferiority in the use of the language is reaching national proportions and threatens to debase our business and professional life.[4]

4. *English is taught more extensively to more pupils than is any other subject.* The prevalence of English instruction in education is graphically demonstrated by the enrollment of 92.9 per cent of all pupils in our high schools in English, as compared to 68 per cent enrolled in

---

[2]Joseph Mersand, *Attitudes Toward English* (Philadelphia: Chilton Press, 1961). All quotations in this section are taken from this survey of the attitudes of national leaders.
[3]Bernard Berelson, *Graduate Education in the United States* (New York: McGraw-Hill Book Company, Inc., 1960), pp. 247-248.
[4]Mersand, *op. cit.*

The enormous teaching problem

the social sciences, 55 per cent in mathematics, and 25 per cent in foreign languages.[5] High schools throughout the country require an average of 3.6 to 3.8 years of English, and the trend to require a full four years is increasing.[6] (No other requirement is so extensive; the study of history and social studies is second with 2.2 to 2.5 years required.) More than 15 per cent of all secondary teachers teach English, compared with 12.9 per cent in mathematics, 12.6 per cent in science, and 11.7 per cent in history and the social studies.[7] The difference does not result from

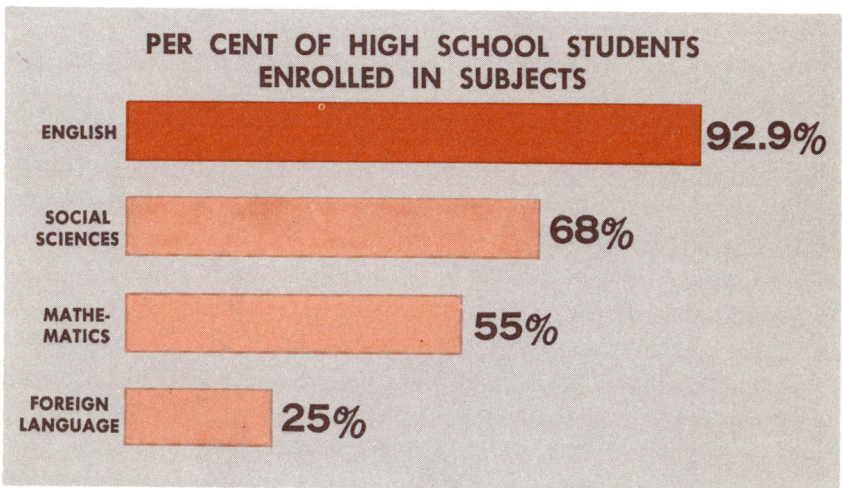

personal choice. Most school programs require children to take English from the first grade to the last, and it is no accident that James B. Conant, in his recent surveys of American high schools, calls strongly, as a first requirement, for four years of English.[8] Virtually all of the 42 millions of students now enrolled in public elementary and secondary schools are studying English under the supervision of more than 900,000 teachers; thousands of others are studying English in independent schools, in colleges, and in universities. Because practically all pupils at all educational levels study English, every change in the nature or size of the school population inevitably affects the teaching of English for better or worse.

---

[5]*Biennial Survey of Education in the United States,* United States Office of Education (Washington, D. C.: U. S. Government Printing Office, 1951), pp. 107 ff.
[6]*Research Bulletin,* National Education Association, Vol. 37, No. 4 (December, 1959), pp. 121-125.
[7]*Teacher Supply and Demand in Public Schools, 1960,* Research Division, National Education Association, April, 1960, p. 10.
[8]James B. Conant, *The American School Today* (New York: McGraw-Hill Book Company, 1958), p. 47, and James B. Conant, *Recommendations for Education in the Junior High School Years* (Princeton, N. J.: Educational Testing Service, 1960), p. 16.

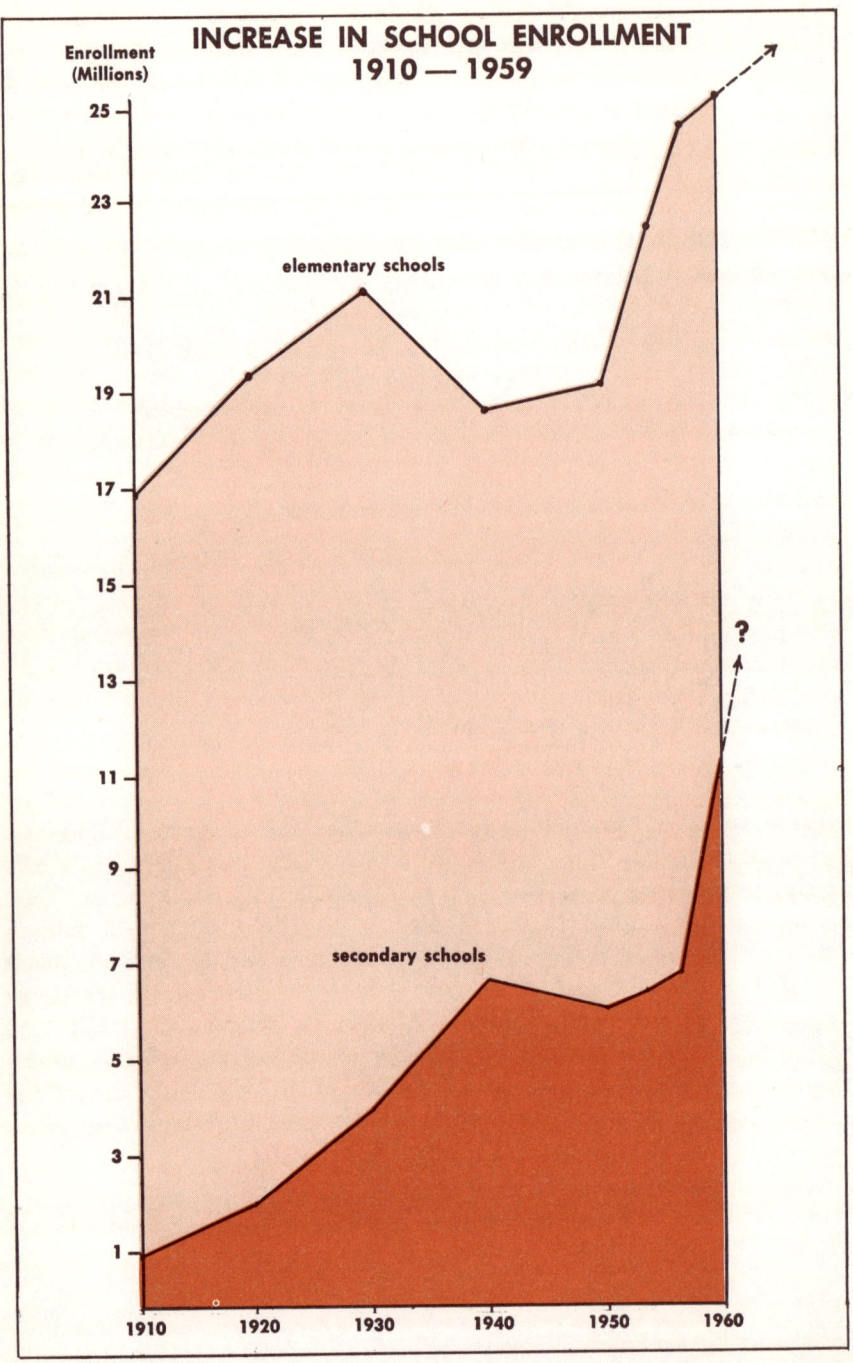

5. *For fifty years the school population has been increasing. The demand for English teachers has increased faster than the number adequately trained—and the 1960's will increase the demand.* Because all

More students require more English teachers

students study English, the rise in school population during the past fifty years has inevitably affected the teaching of English more directly than the teaching of any other subject. From 1910 to 1959, the proportion of the school age population (ages 5 to 17) attending public elementary and secondary schools increased from 74.2 per cent to 83.6 per cent, even while the size of the school age population exploded from about 24 million to 37 million. During this same period, the number enrolled in elementary classrooms (grades 1 to 8) increased from about 17 million to 24 million, while the number enrolled in high schools increased eleven-fold, (from 915,000 to 11,251,000).[9] Despite vigorous efforts to recruit adequately trained teachers in all fields, the gulf between supply and demand continues to widen. Today one-fourth of all elementary school teachers—those responsible for teaching fundamental skills in reading, writing, and language—are *not college* graduates.[10] The number of high school teachers graduated to teach English by the nation's colleges in 1960 was 12 per cent below the number graduated in 1950, despite an increase of about five million in total high school enrollments. And in the number of graduates prepared to teach high school English, 1960 was the best year since 1950![11]

One sampling indicates that during 1958-1959 alone, the demand for trained high school teachers of English outran the supply by 27 per cent.[12] Moreover, expanding enrollments are expected to continue for some time to come. The population of the United States has risen 23.7 per cent since 1946, but the school age population has risen 46.3 per cent. A similar rate of growth should continue in the years ahead.[13] During the past decade, enrollments in public schools have been increasing at an annual average increase of more than one million pupils. These increases are derived largely from children born between 1943 and 1953 at an annual rate ranging from 3,104,000 (1943) to 3,965,000 (1953). Yet beginning in 1954, the annual birth rate has exceeded four million each year. As recent research of the National Education Association

---
[9]*Statistical Summary of Education 1955-56, Biennial Survey of Education in the United States,* U. S. Department of Health, Education, and Welfare, Chapter 1, 1959, pp. 24-25. Statistics for 1959 are reported in *Fall, 1959, Enrollment, Teachers and School Housing,* U. S. Department of Health, Education, and Welfare.

[10]*Teacher Supply and Demand in Public Schools, 1960,* Research Division, National Education Association of the United States, April, 1960, p. 12.

[11]*Ibid.,* p. 11.

[12]See the discussion of these findings on page 34.

[13]*Research Bulletin,* National Education Association, Vol. 36, No. 4 (December, 1959), p. 124.

indicates, in September, 1960, *for the first time,* the elementary schools of this country felt the full impact of four million births six years earlier, and then in only the first of the six grades. But in September, 1965, all six grades of the elementary schools will be serving children born at the rate of four to four and one-half million per year! By September, 1969, our high schools will be deluged with 50 to 70 per cent more students than they can now accommodate.[14] In other words, the demand for adequately prepared elementary and secondary teachers not only continues unabated but will grow even more pressing in the years to come. The total enrollment in elementary schools is expected to increase 13.4 per cent from 1958 to 1965; the enrollment in secondary schools is expected to increase 47 per cent; and college enrollments are expected to increase 40.9 per cent over the 1958 levels.[15] Almost all of these students will be studying English.

These figures we are beginning to get used to. They meet us weekly in sober statements in the press. What we fail to realize is that the expansion has been in process for over thirty years. Figures from a recent U. S. Office of Education report are instructive.[16] They contrast two generations of fifth graders. Of 1,000 pupils who entered the fifth grade in 1924, 612 entered high school, 302 graduated, and 118 went to college. Of 1,000 fifth graders in 1949, 863 entered high school, 581 graduated, and 301 went to college. Note that those entering college represented 30.1 per cent of the original fifth graders and 51.9 per cent of the high school graduates. The so-called "college bound minority" of high school graduates (since about 1953) has in reality been a *"majority,"* and the percentage of high school graduates seeking higher education continues to rise. Preparation of these students by well-educated English teachers is of vital educational importance.

In desperate attempts to cope with the population explosion over the years, thousands of people of good will, but innocent of sound training, have been employed to fill classrooms and teach "English." Who are these teachers? What books have they read? What books are they having their pupils read? Some with only minors in English, many with still less preparation, have managed to hold their pupils' attention in class with all sorts of interesting discussions and materials—but not with English. The

---

[14]*The Pursuit of Excellence—Education and the Future of America,* Special Studies Report V, Rockefeller Brothers Fund (Garden City: Doubleday & Company, Inc., 1958), p. 21.
[15]*Teacher Supply and Demand,* p. 13.
[16]"School Retention Rate Rises," *School Life,* U. S. Office of Education, Vol. 42, No. 5 (January, 1960), pp. 20-21.

content of English accordingly has become increasingly confused and has lost definition. The national waste in time and money reflected in low scores in College Board Examinations and in expenditures upon college programs of "remedial English" is a matter for serious concern.

The drift into the present state of chaos has been subtle and complex; the causes run deep. We must now become aware of the critical problem and muster a national effort to solve it. Assessment of blame is no longer to the point. Explanation, however, is helpful, and alertness to the magnitude of the task that lies before us is imperative.

6. *The old and essential obligations of the English teacher have not changed, but new obligations make his task increasingly difficult.* These new demands have resulted primarily from changes in society, in the composition of the school population, and in the role of communication in the world today.

Different kinds of students

One hundred years ago, many of the people of our country were barred from achieving a full life because they were unable to read and write. Public schools were established to enable—even to require—every person to become literate. From 1870 to 1945 came the task of erecting 30,000 high schools, 100,000 elementary schools, and a thousand colleges; and with this construction came the task of finding a million teachers for thirty million youth from every level of society and every hamlet and crossroads. Those who were teaching English learned to cope, as teachers of English still must learn to cope, with the linguistically privileged and linguistically underprivileged, with the special problems of the bilingual child, with dialectal differences, with the interplay of many accents and vocabularies as children from all segments of life came together in the classroom. The goal of total literacy practically has been reached, and it is no accident that the achievement of literacy has resulted in valuable economic, cultural, and political by-products: the most productive economy in the world, leadership in the sciences and arts, and an increasing extension of democratic rights and responsibilities to most of our citizens.

The need for skills

In recent years, we have tended to be satisfied with mere literacy. Well aware that the scientific, political, and industrial practices of a century ago are too rudimentary for today, we have not faced the fact that simple literacy is not enough. Today industrial firms are spending millions of dollars each year for men, modern counterparts of the ancient scribes, who can rewrite the reports of research engineers into clear and grammatical

English. Businesses are employing the graduates of liberal arts colleges in order to secure executives who can bring a sense of human values to the transactions of the market place. Educators in law and medicine decry the frequent ineptness in reading, writing, and speaking of the young people entering their professions. Colleges are spending too much time and energy on remedial English, working to bring moderately literate students up to the level of skill in communication required for satisfactory college performance. When large numbers of the professionals of our nation are handicapped by ignorance of their mother tongue and unawareness of our humanistic writings, it is obvious that a sizable number of potential professionals and other leaders are lost in the crowd, living beneath their capacities, prevented from fulfilling their potentialities as individuals and from making their contribution to society. In addition, the past quarter century has witnessed steadily

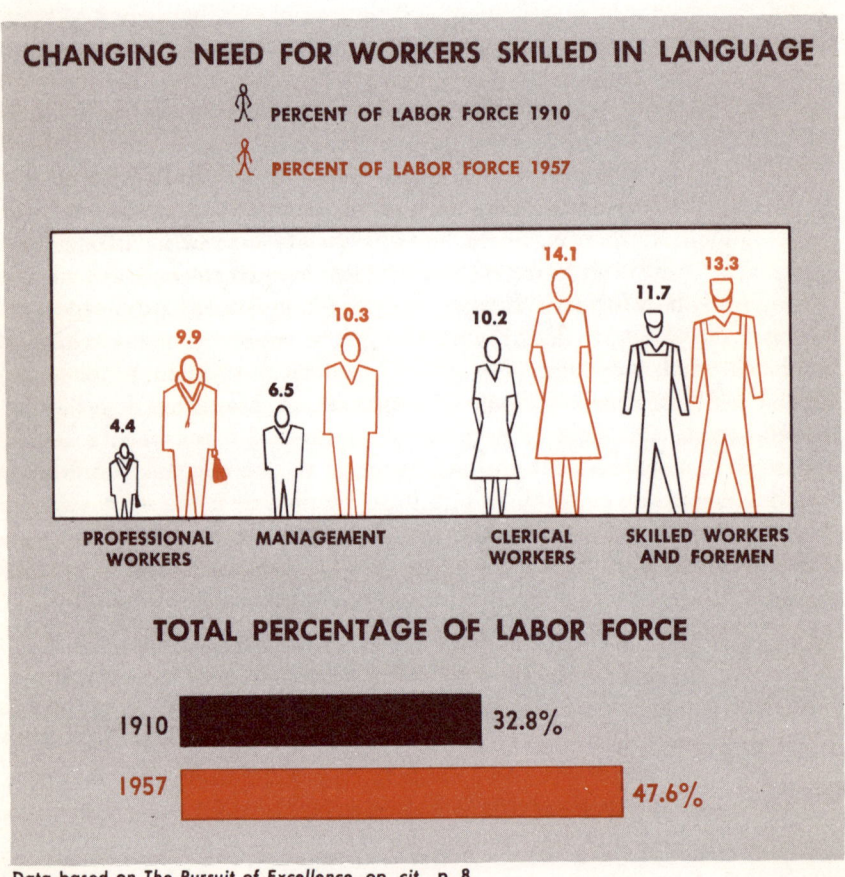

Data based on *The Pursuit of Excellence*, op. cit., p. 8.

increasing demands for workers highly skilled in the use of language; they have been vigorously recruited for public service, for communications, transportation, and other industries, for clerical and white collar positions, and for the professions.[17] Mere literacy is no longer enough in the complicated world in which we live.

The complexity of contemporary life poses still other problems. Our society is increasingly characterized by more corporate and more interdependent organization in all institutional life—each group subdivided into departments, sections, and lines, all of which need to act in unity and harmony. For executives, managers, leaders, clerks, foremen, small businessmen or large, salesmen, distributors, estimators, agents, and government employees—the writing of reports, the framing of directives, the articulation and comprehension of ideas are now essential for accomplishing routine work. Millions of employees today must interpret messages, understand reports, listen and confer, make themselves clear as part of their jobs. Here again mere literacy is no longer enough.

Increasing complexity of life

Increasingly, too, the shift toward greater reliance on oral-aural communication in our technological society produces new concerns for the English teacher. The children and young people in our schools now take casually for granted television, radio, tape recordings, and other instruments of instantaneous communication. These modern media extend popular culture into our living rooms, offering experiences both barren and rich. They inevitably affect many dimensions of our life, and especially of the lives of our young people who, in the words of one critic, "live englobed in a universe of sound . . . which surpasses anything any earlier human culture has known."[18] Our young people need to be educated in both the dangers and the possibilities inherent in the use of these modern media, and inevitably much of this responsibility falls upon the teacher of English, the teacher most concerned about the uses of language and the student's ability to think both critically and imaginatively. Out of these media, too, some special pressures have developed to de-emphasize imaginative literature in our classrooms in favor of sociological documentation. We must not starve our students' imagination or intellect in order to fatten their social conscience.

The impact of modern media of communication

Finally, because the teaching of English has lost clear definition, it has been burdened with an increase in miscellaneous duties and responsi-

---

[17] Clyde B. Moore and William E. Cole, *Sociology in Educational Practice* (New York: Houghton, Mifflin Company, 1952), p. 235.
[18] Walter J. Ong, "Wired for Sound," *College English*, Vol. 21, No. 5 (February, 1960), p. 250.

Proliferation of duties for the English teachers

bilities. Partly perhaps because English is the subject in which virtually all students are enrolled, it has frequently seemed natural to school administrators to consign to English teachers many special responsibilities such as testing, advising, and clerical checking—all desirable and necessary functions but unrelated to any special course. Thus, teachers of English throughout the country expend time and effort on such peripheral tasks as administering tests of vocational preference, lecturing on safety education, and providing orientation for new students.[19]

The ultimate result of all these pressures—the greater heterogeneity of pupils, the increasing complexity of our society, the development of modern media of communication, the proliferation of responsibilities of the English teacher—is that English as a subject is in danger of losing still more its central focus. In too many locales English has become all things to all students. The lines of its discipline have blurred, and the proper path for preparing its teachers has faded.

7. *English and its teachers should focus on the study of language, literature, and composition.* The singular thing about the study of English is that it is a fusion of many elements. In the hands of poor teachers, it is only a hodgepodge. English embraces grammar, good usage, writing, spelling, diction, vocabulary, logic, reading of every kind from magazine articles to poetry. And it attempts to stimulate creation of new ideas, appreciation of quality, good taste, a philosophical temper, exact and efficient communication, and an understanding of values and ideals. With the many pressures now exerted on the teaching of English, a teacher needs great skill to organize all these elements so that they reinforce one another in the student's intellect and imagination. The good teacher, the teacher well prepared in his subject, sees the unity to be found in English and fuses the many elements into a unified subject.

The good teacher sees the unity in English

8. *Poorly prepared teachers of English have created a serious national problem.* Deficiencies in this preparation, dating back many years, have been a major cause of the crisis in English teaching now apparent throughout the country. The present situation is untenable *educationally* because school programs in English seem to have lost their central purpose. It is untenable *economically* because of the tremendous cost of remedial instruction in English throughout our land.[20] It is untenable *politically* because of the increased importance of communication in our society.

Too many ill-prepared teachers

---

[19]Pages 95 and 99 provide factual data on these many responsibilities.
[20]See especially the discussion beginning on page 104.

It is indefensible *culturally* because it threatens to produce a break with the great humanistic tradition.

9. *Probably the greatest single weakness is the lack of articulation in the teaching of English from the elementary school through the college.* English by its nature is a study that requires ten to twelve years (or longer) of continual, rigorous practice under expert guidance—just to develop the skill to write a clear, unified paragraph, or to ferret out the full meaning of an essay, a novel, or a speech. Unlike the study of many other subjects, the study of English is difficult to accelerate. The teacher cannot engage in forced growth and quick coverage in writing and reading, even among the bright, without loss to the pupil. What the teacher must study and understand is the complex, incremental nature of the subject, the way in which language develops, the way in which understanding and appreciation evolve. More than the limited preparation of English teachers stands in the way of achieving sound articulation in English programs. Tens of thousands of separate elementary and secondary school districts plan their own English curriculum; most colleges establish their own requirements and courses without consultation with high schools; diverse organizations work individually and independently to influence the pattern of the English program. Moreover, some secondary schools adopt an elective system in English which makes it possible for students to obtain English credit by enrolling in any one of several related courses. In California alone, courses bearing 217 different titles are classified as English by the state department of education.[21] Under such conditions, continuity in English instruction is virtually impossible. The independence of schools has created a chaotic condition in which strong leadership at the regional, state, and national levels is urgently needed to bring together the diverse, and sometimes discordant, elements into an effective working relationship. Only such strong leadership and coordinated guidance can achieve sound, articulated programs from the first grade to the last.

10. *National concern about the deficiencies in English instruction has become almost commonplace.* Criticisms are voiced in the press daily. When Joseph Mersand, past president of the National Council of Teachers of English, recently studied the attitudes of more than 500 representative college presidents, business executives, lawyers, magazine and newspaper editors, and other professional people, he found a deep-seated national awareness that the improvement of the quality of English

---

[21] Not only speech, drama, and journalism are included but Everyday English, Social English, Junior College English, Vocational English, University English, etc. Cf. *The English Language Arts in California Public High Schools,* Bulletin No. 7, Vol. XXVI, California State Department of Education (September, 1957), pp. 9-11.

teaching will depend on major changes in the conditions under which English is taught. The recommendations from these educated leaders provide a sound base on which a major program may be built: massive efforts on a national scale to provide better prepared teachers of English; increased funds to reduce class size to manageable levels; larger budgets to provide more and better books and instructional materials; higher salaries to attract outstanding teachers.[22]

11. *Coordinated national and state efforts are needed to improve the teaching of English.* The present system of local control of education has been unable to improve the quality of English instruction: its efforts to enlarge the scope of English have been nullified by its inability or unwillingness to change the alarming state into which English has fallen. Local communities seem not to understand (perhaps they are not in a position to understand) that quality in education cannot be achieved without major financial support. For example, if English in secondary schools is to be improved in quality, English teachers must assign more compositions and have more time to read and criticize them. To do so, the number of students they teach must be reduced, in some cases as much as by one-third or even one-half. Across our land the added cost will run to millions. Clearly, serious study must be given to such problems at the state and national levels.

If the preparation in English of secondary teachers and elementary teachers is to be improved, if articulated English programs are to be achieved, then ways must be found to coordinate the separate efforts of organizations, schools, and institutions. Through workshops, institutes, surveys, and conferences, as well as any other means or devices available, our colleges, schools, state departments, teacher organizations, and learned societies must focus their attention on critical problems and make common cause in a major search for solutions. The success of recent national programs in the sciences and modern foreign languages demonstrates what can be accomplished by a nationally financed effort. It is possible for a national program to be instrumental in mobilizing local resources in a way that disparate, separate authorities could never do and to tap educational leadership in ways never before thought possible. One of the major recommendations of the forums at the Golden Anniversary White House Conference on Children and Youth is that a National Humanities Foundation be established to coordinate efforts in the various humanistic disciplines and to provide leadership in sponsoring research and study designed to advance the science of man.[23] It

---

[22]Mersand, *op. cit.*
[23]*Committee Report on Foreign Findings,* Golden Anniversary White House Conference on Children and Youth (Washington, D. C., Government Printing Office, 1960), p. 1.

seems impossible to correct the basic weaknesses in English instruction under existing multitudinous administrative organizations, isolated authorities, and small town school referendums. Some examples of what can be accomplished in national leadership, without endangering local control, are already before us. For instance, the impact which the United States Congress may have in providing for special services and regional coordination in a subject was dramatized when, as a result of the passage of the National Defense Education Act of 1958, the number of state supervisors in modern languages increased from eight to forty-one.[24] At present only six states employ supervisors in English, even though most states regularly employ such specialists in home economics, trade and industrial arts, and other nonacademic areas. Such leadership at the state level can promote articulation of programs in English from the kindergarten through the high school and influence articulation between the high school and the college. Or, for a different approach on the national level, consider the effect of the 1956 Ann Arbor Conference on the teaching of English as a foreign language. This conference, supported by the Ford Foundation and sponsored by the Linguistic Society and the Committee on International Exchange of Persons of the Conference Board of Associated Research Councils, brought together for the first time the linguists and the nonlinguistically trained teachers of English as a foreign language. Its impact upon the methods of teaching and the preparation of teachers of English as a foreign language has already been significant; its lasting contribution has been dramatized by the organizing of the Center for Applied Linguistics in Washington as a branch of the Modern Language Association of America.

When we recognize that education is vital to the survival of freedom, we become sensitive to our responsibilities as free individuals and can appraise ourselves rigorously as a society. We come to think of brain power and intelligence as we think of forests and river basins—as a national resource to be conserved and developed, not wasted. In the midst of our personal concerns, we suddenly look at the public domain and wonder why we have neglected it when it is so essential to our individual existence. Education is part of the public domain, the national interest; English is the core of public education. So busy are we in the pursuit of private dreams and pleasures, in getting and spending, in seeking to achieve personal goals of wealth or well-being, so conditioned have we become to obsolescence, to tearing down and throwing away—that we have not heeded pressing needs now suddenly essential to survival. "The issue at its simplest," writes Barbara Ward in

---

[24]"State Supervisors in Science, Mathematics, and Modern Foreign Languages," *School Life,* U. S. Office of Education, Vol. 42, No. 5 (March, 1960), pp. 28-29.

the *New York Times,* "is the question whether the United States is spending too much on its private necessities and enjoyments and, as a result, skimping the broad public needs and services that are vital to its very social and national existence."[25]

Petty factional strife, selfish interest, or stunted vision in thousands of our school elections has already hampered English instruction for many years to come, has thrust many students into the hands of incompetent teachers or of competent teachers who are teaching under appalling conditions.[26] The fate of our democracy now rests on the way we develop our manpower. And English can, in transmitting the humanistic tradition, help vitalize democracy, and, in developing the art and skill of communication, help assure its lasting strength.

---

[25]*New York Times,* May 8, 1960.
[26]The nature of these conditions is discussed on pages 43-104.

PART III

The Status of English Teaching Today

- THE NEED FOR MORE TEACHERS OF ENGLISH
- THE NEED FOR BETTER TEACHERS OF ENGLISH
  - A Standard of Preparation to Teach English
  - State Certification Regulations for Teaching English
  - The Preparation of the Elementary Teacher in English
  - The English Language Preparation of Secondary Teachers of English
  - The Preparation in Literature of Secondary Teachers of English
- THE NEED FOR BETTER TEACHING CONDITIONS
  - The Conditions under Which English Is Taught
  - The Inadequacy of School Library and Book Resources
  - The Cost of Remedial Instruction at the College Level
  - High Schools That Produce Superior English Students
- THE NEED FOR BETTER AND MORE BASIC RESEARCH IN ENGLISH

III

The Status of English Teaching Today

What are the conditions under which English is taught in this country? Why is vigorous national leadership so urgently needed? A review of the known facts about the present conditions leads inescapably to four conclusions:

We need more teachers of English.

We need better teachers of English.

We need better teaching conditions.

We need better and more basic research in English and the teaching of English.

Each of these imperative needs is discussed in this section.

THE NEED FOR MORE TEACHERS OF ENGLISH

> **Highlights**
>
> The shortage of teachers has remained unchanged for two years and shows no sign of decreasing.
>
> One-fourth of all elementary teachers are not college graduates.
>
> The demand for secondary teachers of English is outrunning the supply by 27 per cent.
>
> Only 40 to 60 per cent of the teachers of high school English have completed college majors in English.
>
> Colleges report an acute shortage of instructors trained in linguistics and composition.

At the opening of the 1959 school year, an estimated 2,819,000 students in public schools—one in every 13—were being taught by teachers who did not meet the minimum certification standards established by the various states. From 1958 to 1959 the number of substandard teachers in secondary schools increased by 19.1 per cent; the number of substandard elementary teachers, by 1.7 per cent. A total of 98,800 teachers—29,300 secondary and 69,500 elementary—did not meet even the minimum standards established as legal for teaching by various states. These are official figures reported in 1959 by state departments of education. The nation's schools opened in the fall of 1960 needing 135,000 qualified teachers, a figure which has remained unchanged for two years and shows no sign of decreasing! This is the appalling shortage which faces the public schools of the nation.[1]

Shortages continue unabated

The Supply of Elementary Teachers

During the past decade, as the need for elementary teachers has been widely publicized, recruitment efforts have resulted in a progressive increase in the number of persons planning to teach at this level. Al-

---

[1] Samuel Scholoss and Carol Joy Hobson, *Enrollment, Teachers, and School Housing*, Circular No. 604, U. S. Department of Health, Education, and Welfare, 1959, p. 4.

Many substandard teachers

though *numbers* have increased, the *percentage* of graduating seniors preparing to teach has not risen materially. Moreover, evidence presented subsequently in this report indicates that many credentialed elementary teachers lack genuine competence in the subjects they must teach.[2] The high American birth rate continues; the result—swollen school enrollments and an acute, unabated shortage of elementary teachers. Any notion that this shortage has been reduced or "ironed out" is entirely spurious. The fact is that one-fourth of all elementary teachers are not yet college graduates and that as many as 200,000 have completed no more than two years of college.[3]

Crowded classes and part day sessions which reduce the effectiveness of each child's education result from the teacher shortage. Fully 83.3 per cent of all elementary children are now enrolled in classes containing more than 25 students,[4] the size considered by most professional specialists in English to be desirable for effective teaching.[5] If 95,000 qualified elementary and secondary teachers are needed to replace those permitted to teach with substandard credentials, at least 100,000 more must be found to reduce the oversize classes.[6]

Taught by substandard teachers under substandard conditions, children almost inevitably receive a substandard education. Development of skill in reading and skill in the use of language, to mention only two areas, depends on a sound, rigorous elementary program. In view of the shockingly inadequate conditions in many elementary schools during the past decade, many children now entering high school are more adequately prepared in fundamentals than the nation has any reason to expect.

The Supply of Secondary Teachers of English

The need to recruit competent teachers of secondary English is also urgent. Despite a recent increase in the number of college graduates preparing to teach English—an increase which happily climbed to 15 per cent in 1960 over 1959—the demand for teachers of English far exceeds the supply. For example, last year a special sampling of 27 states indicated that only 3,612 secondary teachers of English were certified to meet a demand for 4,679 positions of English, the need here outrunning the supply by more than 27 per cent during a single year.[7]

---

[2]See pages 48-60.
[3]*Teacher Supply and Demand in Public Schools, 1960*, Research Division, National Education Association of the United States, April, 1960. p. 5. Also, "The Teacher Shortage Analyzed," *Research Bulletin*, National Education Association, Vol. 38, No. 3 (October, 1960), p. 71.
[4]*Ibid.*, p. 12.
[5]See pages 96-98 for evidence to support this assertion.
[6]Scholoss and Hobson, p. 4.
[7]All figures taken from *Teacher Supply and Demand in Public Schools, 1960*, Research Division, NEA, p. 10.

An estimated 15.5 per cent of all teachers are teachers of English; yet in 1960 (a good year for recruitment of English teachers) only 11.7 per cent of the new prospective teachers entering the teaching profession were preparing to teach in this field.

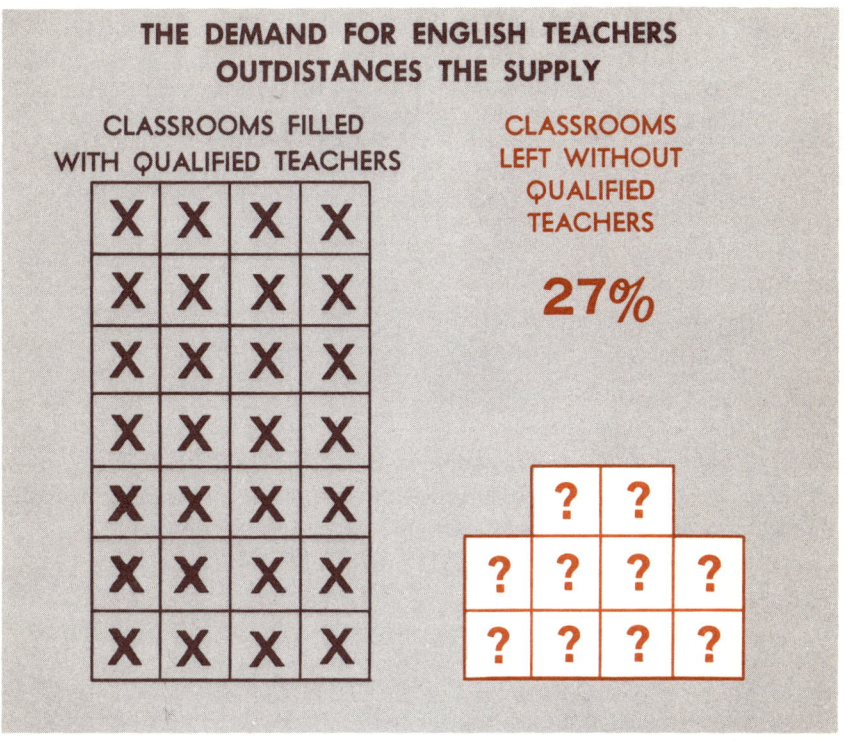

When certified teachers are not available, someone must be found to man the classrooms. Each year thousands of substandard teachers are employed on an emergency basis in secondary and elementary classrooms.

Almost half lack teaching majors

The shortage of adequately educated teachers of English has led to the assignment of persons to teach English who are really specialists in other academic, sometimes even nonacademic, subjects. Exact figures on the number of substandard teachers are not available, some state superintendents reporting that they lack this information themselves. (The need for more adequate statistical surveys of such information is evident.) The data available from two states suggest that not over 50 to 60 per cent of the persons teaching English in our junior and senior high schools have been certified with teaching majors in the subject. Items:

In Virginia, only 41.1 per cent of teachers of English possess a major in English. An additional 18.6 per cent possess a major in speech, dramatics, or some related field but apparently not with depth in subject matter sufficient for a regular English credential.[8]

In California, 52.79 per cent of the English teachers in four-year high schools, 58.55 per cent of those in three-year high schools, but only 32.09 per cent of those in junior high schools report majors in English (and these figures include majors with mixed combination of English, speech, dramatics, and journalism).[9]

In Illinois, 52 per cent of the teachers surveyed in 1954 reported English as their major, and an additional 14 per cent majored in a combination of English, speech, and journalism.[10]

In Indiana, 62 per cent of the high school teachers of English possess majors in the area, according to a recent survey.[11]

In Wisconsin, 60 per cent of the secondary teachers of English responding to a questionnaire report that they have been prepared as English majors (24 semester hours of English).[12]

If these conditions apply elsewhere—and there appears to be little reason to suspect that they do not—between 40 and 60 per cent of the English in our public junior and senior high schools is being taught by teachers who lack even the minimal training required for a major in English. And, as a later section of this report will make clear, many of those with majors in English fall considerably below qualifications for teaching English considered to be reasonable and necessary.[13]

The Supply of College Teachers of English

Colleges and universities, only just beginning to feel the impact of the swollen enrollments which have overwhelmed elementary and secondary schools for a decade, are becoming increasingly concerned about the expected shortage of well-educated college teachers of English in future years. Some evidence already suggests that the preparation of new college teachers is less adequate than it used to be; for example, one survey reports that since 1953-1954 the number of those holding doctoral degrees among newly employed college teachers has declined

Acute shortage in language

---

[8] Foster B. Gresham, *The Teaching of English in Virginia High Schools* (Farmville, Virginia: Virginia Association of Teachers of English, 1958), p. 9.
[9] *The English Language Arts in California Public High Schools,* Bulletin No. 7, Vol. XXVI, California State Department of Education (September, 1957), p. 13.
[10] Charles Willard and John D. Mees, "A Study of the Preparation of Present Teachers of English in Illinois and Their Recommendations for an Improved Training Program," *Illinois English Bulletin,* Vol. 41, No. 8 (May, 1954), p. 9.
[11] Ingrid M. Strom, *Teaching Load of Teachers of English in Indiana,* Bulletin, Vol. 32, No. 3, School of Education, Indiana University (May, 1956), p. 25.
[12] Reported by John Searles in Alfred Grommon (ed.), *The Preparation of the Teacher of the English Language Arts* (Champaign, Ill.: The National Council of Teachers of English [in preparation]).
[13] See pages 60 and 75.

25.2 per cent.[14] At present, shortages are more apparent in some areas of specialization than in others. A 1959 survey of approximately one hundred college and university departments of English revealed a serious shortage of teachers qualified to offer instruction in language and linguistics.[15] (A majority of universities and one-third of the smaller institutions reported that too few candidates were available in these fields.) This condition is especially disturbing because information presented later in this report indicates a need to increase college offerings in language and linguistics.[16] Fully qualified college teachers must certainly be found if proposals to improve the education of school teachers are to succeed.

Colleges and universities also report shortages of qualified instructors in other important areas of English teaching. Good teachers of advanced composition and creative writing are difficult to find; so are persons prepared to offer work in methods of teaching English. Offerings in these areas are essential to the education of teachers of English.

A special need exists for obtaining well-prepared college teachers of freshman composition. Most colleges report no difficulty in obtaining enough teachers for freshman classes, largely because every new instructor is regularly assigned such responsibilities regardless of his interests and aspirations. What does create difficulty is his lack of preparation and of motivation for such teaching; the teaching-assistant graduate student and the young Ph.D. assigned to such work may expect ninety per cent of their first six years of teaching to be in beginning composition, yet the typical Ph.D. program includes almost no work in rhetoric and language.[17] Warner G. Rice, chairman of the committee which surveyed needs at the college level, observes that:

> These new teachers can teach grammar formally, but composition, the actual composing process, is something which is beyond them. Thus, although the supply of elementary composition teachers is adequate, they are not really prepared to do what most of them are going to have to do when they go into their first years of college teaching, which is precisely to teach freshman English.

The need for college English instructors in all fields will increase in proportion to college enrollments. At the present time, however, the shortages are serious primarily in areas related to the teaching of lan-

---

[14] *The Pursuit of Excellence-Education and the Future of America,* Special Studies Project Report V (Garden City: Doubleday & Company, Inc., 1958), p. 2.
[15] This survey was conducted during 1959-60 by the Committee on the Education of College Teachers of English of the National Council of Teachers of English, Warner G. Rice, chairman. Results will be reported in a future issue of *College English.* The information in this section is based on this survey.
[16] See page 74.
[17] *The Basic Issues in the Teaching of English,* presented by members of the American Studies Association, College English Association, the Modern Language Association, and the National Council of Teachers of English, 1959, p. 13.

Limited assistance for graduate study guage and composition. To encourage more graduate students to prepare for teaching college English, financial inducements must be increased. A recently concluded survey of graduate students in arts and sciences reveals a clear differential between the stipends available in natural sciences and those available in the humanities and the social sciences. At the present time a graduate student in natural science from the lower 40 per cent of his graduating class has a better chance for a stipend than a graduate student in the humanities (or social sciences) from the top 20 per cent of his class.[18] Greater financial inducements will be mandatory if the nation is to recruit a greater number of teachers from the most highly qualified graduates.

A Continuing Demand for Teachers of English

The critical demand for teachers of English will continue into the foreseeable future. Predictions of increasing enrollments, reported earlier in this document,[19] suggest the problem ahead. As the 1959 Rockefeller Report on education states, "The number of new school teachers needed in the next decade is between one-third and one-half of all four-year graduates of every kind in the same period. Since only one out of every four or five college graduates becomes a teacher, the magnitude of the problem is apparent, even allowing the fact that recent college graduates are not the only source of supply. The danger of a decline in the quality of our core of teachers is obvious."[20]

---

[18]James A. Davis, "The Financial Situation of American Arts and Science Graduate Students, Highlights and Major Findings," National Opinion Research Center, University of Chicago, 1960. p. 4 (mimeographed).
[19]See page 22.
[20]*The Pursuit of Excellence-Education and the Future of America*, Special Studies Project Report V (Garden City: Doubleday & Company, Inc., 1958), p. 23.

THE NEED FOR BETTER TEACHERS OF ENGLISH

Our profession today needs not only more teachers, but, especially, more *highly qualified* teachers. To bring unity to a subject as complex as English, a teacher must be carefully prepared.[1] Attempts to attract into teaching increasing numbers of students of high academic competence must be paralleled by efforts to improve existing programs of preparation. This section suggests a standard of preparation for those preparing to teach English, then reviews existing certification regulations and college programs for those who plan to teach. The discussion is presented in five parts:

A Standard of Preparation to Teach English
State Certification Regulations for Teaching English
The Preparation of the Elementary Teacher in English
The English Language Preparation of the Secondary Teachers of English
The Preparation in Literature of the Secondary Teachers of English

A STANDARD OF PREPARATION TO TEACH ENGLISH

What is a good standard of preparation to teach English? Basic to all efforts to upgrade the quality of teaching is the identification of competent teachers. To that end, a special committee of the National Council of Teachers of English has suggested the essential qualifications of an English teacher—in the elementary school, the secondary school, the college, or the university.[2] Teaching by persons who cannot meet this standard will not produce the communication skills or the sense of human values needed so urgently in our nation. Certainly both beginning and experienced teachers must, through study and practical experience, work further to achieve and maintain the highest qualifications. The standard outlined represents only the quality of education in English needed by teachers to achieve the goals identified in the foregoing chapter; it is realistic and can be met.

A standard for teacher preparation

While the committee's statement assumes a common basis for teachers of English, it allows for appropriate specialization to teach in each of the several positions from the elementary school to the university. The capable, industrious student should fulfill the requirements of the statement by the end of his baccalaureate or master's degree, to the extent that these apply to his preparation as a teacher in the elementary or

---

[1] See the discussion on page 26.
[2] This statement was initially prepared by the Committee on Preparation and Certification of Teachers, National Council of Teachers of English, Eugene E. Slaughter, chairman. The standards are supported by the committee preparing this document and by other leaders of the Council.

secondary school, and by the end of his doctoral study as they relate to college teaching. Let's assume that our prospective English teacher has good opportunities to learn language and literature during his childhood and youth. Much of the basic knowledge of English as his native language—which he understands, reads, speaks, and writes—he should have by the time he enters college. Likewise, by that time he should have read a number of major works that belong to English and American literature and some foreign pieces in the original language or English translation. He should consequently have developed a fair ability to judge and a taste to choose among literary works. During his four or five years of collegiate study, he should extend and sharpen his fundamental knowledge of the English language and literature and should acquire the special knowledge of English, together with the science and art of teaching it, which he will need for his work in the elementary or secondary school. If he intends to teach in the college or university, he should shape his program of studies to that end.

Knowledge of language and literature

Those who subscribe to this statement hope that the teacher of English (1) has the personal qualities which make an effective teacher, (2) has received a well-balanced education, including knowledge of a foreign language and a basic grounding in science, mathematics, the social sciences, and the arts, (3) has received the appropriate training in psychology and professional education, and (4) has dedicated himself to humanistic values.

A Standard of Preparation to Teach English

I. The teacher of English should have a certain fundamental and specialized knowledge of the English language and its literature, together with certain abilities and skills which enable him to perform expertly in his discipline.

    A. In language, he should have:

        1. A fundamental knowledge of the historical development and present character of the English language: phonology (phonetics and pho-

nemics), morphology, syntax, vocabulary (etymology and semantics), the relations of language and society.
2. A specialized knowledge of the English language which is appropriate to the teacher's particular field of interest and responsibility.
3. An informed command of the arts of language—rhetoric and logic; ability to speak and write language which is not only unified, coherent, and correct but also responsible, appropriate to the situation, and stylistically effective.

B. In literature, he should have:
1. A reading background of major literary works which emphasize the essential dignity of the individual man. This background:
   a. Implies a knowledge of major works, writers, forms, themes, and movements of the literature of the English-speaking people.
   b. Reflects intensive study of many literary pieces.
   c. Includes familiarity with some of the outstanding literary works in English translation, or in the original language, of the Greek, Roman, Norse, Italian, French, Spanish, German, Slavic, and Oriental peoples.
2. A specialized knowledge of whatever writers and literary works, forms, themes, media, and movements are appropriate to the teacher's particular field of interest and responsibility.
3. An ability to analyze and evaluate independently the various forms of imaginative literature as well as the utilitarian forms of verbal expression, and the insight to use suitable critical approaches in order to discover their literary and human values.

II. The teacher of English should have certain abilities and knowledge which belong to the science and the art of teaching language and literature.

A. These abilities include:
   1. The ability to envision how his students may develop their potentialities through the study of language and literature.
   2. The ability to excite their interest and direct their learning.
   3. The ability to help them understand and use English practically and creatively.
   4. The ability to elevate their taste and critical powers.
   5. The ability to lead them to a perception of human problems and an appreciation of human values.
   6. The ability to evaluate their progress and the efficacy of his own methods.

B. These abilities presuppose not only the fundamental but also the specialized knowledge and skills of the English language and literature which the teacher needs to fulfill his professional responsibility.

C. These abilities imply knowledge of the philosophies of education and the psychologies of learning as they relate to the study and teaching of the English language and its literature. Such knowledge:
   1. Reveals how an individual unfolds and grows through his use and understanding of language and literature.
   2. Supplies the teacher with a variety of methods for use in teaching his students the skills and arts which are appropriate to their level of attainment in English.
   3. Informs the teacher of the relation which each phase or level has to the total school, college, and university program.
   4. Includes an awareness of the basic issues in the teaching of English.

STATE CERTIFICATION REGULATIONS FOR TEACHING ENGLISH IN ELEMENTARY AND SECONDARY SCHOOLS

> **Highlights**
>
> States differ widely on the qualifications for elementary and secondary teaching.
>
> Ten states certify elementary teachers who do not possess a bachelor's degree.
>
> Nineteen states do not specify any requirement in English for elementary certification; twenty-one do not report a definite requirement in reading, children's literature, or methods of teaching the language arts.
>
> A median of 16 to 18 semester hours of English is required nationally as minimum preparation for teachers assigned classes in English.
>
> In sixteen states not more than 12 semester hours are required for the part time teaching of English.

In virtually all states the minimum requirements to teach in public school are established by state departments or state boards of education. These state requirements are both quantitative and qualitative but tend to emphasize general qualifications of teachers rather than specific standards in a subject. Generally, state agencies require all teachers to receive a liberal education with one or more concentrations in subjects to be taught and a professional education that includes the psychological and sociological foundations of the teaching-learning process, teaching methods, and student teaching. They attempt to provide for quality by requiring certain necessary portions of the total preparation to be in courses designed to develop special competencies. Some states use proficiency examinations as a substitute for a prescribed course that the teacher candidate has not included in his college preparation. A few states require the candidate to make a designated score on a standardized national teacher examination in order to receive a certificate; other states encourage him to include such a score in his personnel file; still others require, for renewal of a certificate, that he pass a locally prepared examination or earn a minimum number of additional college credits. An increasing tendency is to require that the teacher-preparing institution be accredited by state, regional, and national agencies and that it recommend its graduates as to character and competency before they are issued certificates. States are able to enforce their certification requirements through accreditation policies and control of funds granted to public schools, threatening the withdrawal of accreditation or withholding of money from schools that do not comply.[3]

How much college work is required to teach in elementary and secondary schools? The answer is presented in the following table.

AMOUNT OF COLLEGE WORK REQUIRED FOR REGULAR CERTIFICATION

(Expressed in the Number of States and Territories Reporting Requirement)

Amount of College Work Required	Elementary School Certification		Secondary School Certification	
	Lowest Regular Elementary School Certificate	Standard Elementary School Certificate	Lowest Regular Secondary School Certificate	Standard Secondary School Certificate
Bachelor's Degree Plus One Year	0	5	3	8
Bachelor's Degree	42	47	49	44
Three Years	2	0	0	0
Two Years	6	0	0	0
One Year	2	0	0	0
	52	52	52	52

Of the 52 "states" (defined to include the District of Columbia and Puerto Rico here and throughout the remainder of this section), 42 require a bachelor's degree for the *lowest regular elementary school* certificate, 2 (Alaska and Maine) require three years of college, 6 (Colorado, Missouri, Montana, Puerto Rico, South Dakota, and Wisconsin) require two years of college, and 2 (Nebraska and North Dakota) require one year of college. For the *standard elementary school* certificate, 47 states require a bachelor's degree, and 5 (Connecticut, Hawaii, Indiana, Kentucky, and Washington) require a bachelor's degree plus a fifth year of college work. For the *lowest regular secondary school* certificate, 49 states re-

---

[3]W. E. Armstrong and T. M. Stinnett, *A Manual on Certification Requirements* (National Education Association of the United States, 1959); John H. Fisher, "We Look to the High Schools," *College English*, XVI (March, 1955), 362-365; "Certification of High School Teachers," *College English*, XIX (May, 1958), 344-348; and "1960 Certification Requirements," *College English*, XXII (January, 1961), 267-271; Eugene E. Slaughter, "The Use of Examinations for State Certification of Teachers," *The Journal of Teacher Education*, XI (June, 1960), 231-238, and an unpublished survey of 1960 certification to teach English in the elementary school. These publications and studies are also the source of data on certification which appear hereafter without citation.

quire the bachelor's degree, and 3 (Arizona, California, and the District of Columbia) require a bachelor's degree plus a fifth year of college work. For the *standard secondary school* certificate, 44 states require the bachelor's degree, and 8 (Arizona, California, Connecticut, District of Columbia, Indiana, New York, Oregon, and Washington) require the bachelor's degree plus a fifth year of college work.

How many semester hours of work in general education, professional teacher education, and English are required to teach in the elementary school? The data are summarized in the following table.

STATE SPECIFICATIONS CONCERNING THE AMOUNT OF GENERAL EDUCATION, PROFESSIONAL TEACHER EDUCATION, AND ENGLISH (INCLUDING IN SOME CASES SUCH RELATED SUBJECTS AS SPEECH, DRAMATICS, AND JOURNALISM) REQUIRED FOR THE LOWEST DEGREE-BASED ELEMENTARY SCHOOL CERTIFICATE

(Expressed in Semester Hours of College Credit)

	General Education	Professional Teacher Education	English
High	104	36	18
Median	45	21	6
Low	16	16	0

State requirements for teaching in an elementary school, expressed in semester hours of college credit, range from 16 to 104, median 45, in general education; range from 16 to 36, median 21, in professional teacher education; range from 0 to 18, median 6, in the area of English, journalism, speech, and dramatics. The great variation in requirements from state to state points to widespread confusion and uncertainty concerning desirable qualifications of elementary teachers and to a need for considered national guidance.

The *median* state credential requirement in English for an elementary teaching certificate is only six semester hours. Although the teaching of English is one of the elementary teacher's major responsibilities, nineteen states specify no college work in English; eight require one year, the equivalent of freshman English; sixteen require up to two years or twelve semester hours of English; nine states require more than two years.

Little work in English specified

Specialized subject courses concerned with the teaching of the language arts in the elementary school are not uniformly required. Nine states require work in methods of teaching reading; fourteen require work in children's literature; only twenty-two specify a general study of the English language arts as a requirement for obtaining a certificate to teach English in the elementary school. Twenty-one states do not report a definite requirement in reading methods, children's literature, or the English language arts in the elementary school, even though they may require a general methods course.

Clearly the pattern of courses cannot alone guarantee the proficiency of the teacher; states and teacher training institutions need reasonable flexibility in planning programs. Yet the diversity of requirements indicated here and the failure of many states to specify even a minimal requirement in English are matters for concern.

How many semester hours of work in general education, professional teacher education, and English are required to teach English in the secondary school? This table presents the data.

STATE SPECIFICATIONS CONCERNING THE AMOUNT OF GENERAL EDUCATION, PROFESSIONAL TEACHER EDUCATION, AND ENGLISH SUBJECT MATTER REQUIRED TO TEACH ENGLISH IN A SECONDARY SCHOOL

(Expressed in Semester Hours of College Credit)

	General Education	Professional Teacher Education	Minimum English Subject Matter	
			To Teach English as Full Load	To Teach English as Part Load
High	104	27	30	30
Median	40	18	18	16
Low	25	12	12	0

State requirements to teach English in a secondary school range from 25 semester hours of college credits to 104, median 40, in general education; range from 12 to 27, median 18, in professional teacher education; range from 12 to 30, median 18, in the area of English, journalism, speech, and dramatics for teaching English as a full load; range from 0 to 30, median 16, in the area for teaching English as a part load. The requirements for a part load are reported because many states distinguish between those who teach part time (one or two classes of English) and those who are assigned English as their major load. The great variation in all requirements reflects the present confusion on the part of state educational

Variation suggests confusion

authorities concerning the education needed by prospective teachers of English and underscores the importance of national and regional efforts to assist in defining essential requirements. The variation from state to state becomes even clearer by examining the data in the following table.

AMOUNT OF ENGLISH (INCLUDING IN SOME CASES SUCH RELATED SUBJECTS AS SPEECH, DRAMATICS, AND JOURNALISM) REQUIRED AS A MINIMUM TO TEACH SECONDARY SCHOOL ENGLISH

(Expressed in Semester Hours of College Credit and Number of States Reporting Requirement)

Number of States and Territories Reporting Requirement

Semester Hours College Credit	English, etc., *Minimum* to Teach English as Full Load	English, etc., *Minimum* to Teach English as Part Load
30	4	2
28	1	1
24	18	13
20	2	2
18	8	7
16	3	2
15	10	9
12	4	3
10	0	1
9	0	2
8	0	1
6	0	2
Unspecified	2	7
Total	52	52
Median	18 sem. hrs.	16 sem. hrs.

Thus a median of 16 to 18 semester hours is all that is required by state certifying agencies to teach English as a full load or a part load. In 16 states not more than twelve semester hours are required for part time teaching, the equivalent of only a one-year course beyond freshman English. In seven states no minimum is specified clearly. State credential regulations offer no assurance that teachers certified to teach English will be adequately prepared. Still, during recent years, many states have attempted to strengthen credential requirements in English. For example, between 1954 and 1960, twenty-four states increased subject requirements in English.[4] Although the median requirement remains only 16 to 18

Median secondary requirement is 16-18 hours

---
[4] John H. Fisher, "1960 Certification Requirements," *College English*, January, 1961, 267-271.

47

semester hours, the trend suggests the readiness of state certification agencies to consider ways of strengthening present programs.

Summary

Present state certification regulations do not ensure that teachers certified to teach English are well prepared. Although, perhaps rightfully, state regulations tend not to prescribe detailed programs of study, the variations in requirements from state to state suggest the need for defining minimum standards of preparation which should be generally required. Most states' regulations establish only general requirements and encourage each teacher education institution to develop its own curriculum for educating prospective teachers. As the sections following will indicate, the programs developed in many institutions often fail to equip graduates with the necessary knowledge and skills.

THE PREPARATION OF THE ELEMENTARY TEACHER IN ENGLISH

Highlights

Virtually all students preparing to teach in the elementary school are required to *pass* freshman English.

The typical college requires students preparing to teach elementary school to complete only two or three semesters of work in language or literature in addition to the freshman course.

Two-thirds of the colleges do not require future elementary teachers to complete more than five semester hours of work in reading and language arts at the elementary level. Thus, except for work in freshman composition, the average college requires that only ten per cent of the total program be spent on English or the teaching of English.

More than 94 per cent of the colleges fail to require work in the English language. In addition, almost half of the colleges fail to require a course on teaching the English language. The preparation of elementary teachers for teaching students to write and speak seems very limited indeed.

The instruction in the fundamental skills of language is a crucial goal of elementary education. Unless a teacher is prepared in English, unless he understands both language and literature and how to teach reading, writing, and the other skills of language, he can scarcely be effective in his teaching. This survey of the preparation of the elementary teacher in English focuses on only one aspect of the teacher's total preparation. Obviously the elementary teacher must also be prepared in other subjects and in professional education; this study concentrates only on one vital area of his preparation. However, the central position of language teaching in the elementary school makes especially crucial each teacher's competence in English.

Scope of the Study

During late September, 1960, a special questionnaire was sent to the chairman of the department of education in 2,000 colleges on an unselected list. Within forty-five days, 984 questionnaires had been returned, 49.7 per cent of the total. Four hundred and twenty-five responses were from schools which did not prepare elementary school teachers. The valid remaining responses as of November 15, 1960, totaled 569. The information asked in the questionnaire included:

The number of elementary teachers graduated in June, 1960.

The extent to which elementary teachers complete a subject major outside of education.

The extent to which elementary candidates are permitted to substitute two subject minors for a subject major.

The prevalence of freshman English or its equivalent as a requirement for elementary teachers.

The number of semester hours in English required of such students.

The courses in literature required of such students.

The courses in language and composition required of such students.

The extent of course requirements in oral interpretation of literature, speech, speech correction, creative dramatics, children's literature.

The number of credit hours required in courses dealing with the teaching of reading and the language arts.

Prevalence of course requirements in methods of teaching, in methods of teaching language arts, or in general methods.

The content of the required course in general methods with respect to the teaching of reading and the language arts.

Distribution of Responses

Responses were classified into categories based on size and type of institution. Responses tabulated in category A are from general liberal arts colleges and universities enrolling more than 1,000 full time students (according to the 1960 World Almanac); responses tabulated as B are from liberal arts institutions enrolling 301 to 1,000 students; category C includes responses from liberal arts institutions with fewer than 301 students. Category T is used for teachers colleges. The distribution of institutions on which this survey is based is as follows:

			Per cent
Liberal Arts Institutions	A	268	47.1%
Liberal Arts Institutions	B	230	40.3
Liberal Arts Institutions	C	31	5.4
Teachers Colleges	T	40	7.2
Total		569	

In this sampling, the percentage of responses from teachers colleges is larger than in the other surveys. Even so, eighty-seven per cent of the responses are from general colleges and universities with liberal arts programs.

NUMBER OF ELEMENTARY TEACHERS GRADUATED IN JUNE, 1960

	Less than 10 Graduates	10-25 Grads.	26-50 Grads.	Over 50 Grads.	Not Given	Total
A	11	55	60	108	34	268
B	31	117	42	18	22	230
C	12	10	1	1	7	31
T	1	7	9	22	1	40
Total	55	189	112	149	64	569
Per cent	9.7%	33.2%	19.6%	26.2%	11.3%	

The teacher training institutions reporting in this survey are of varying sizes. Approximately forty per cent graduated 25 or fewer elementary teachers in June, 1960. An almost equal number reported graduating 26 or more elementary teachers in June, 1960.

DO ELEMENTARY TEACHERS COMPLETE A SUBJECT MAJOR OUTSIDE OF EDUCATION?				
	Yes	% of total responses[5]	No	%[5]
A	85	31.7%	183	68.3%
B	78	33.9	152	66.1
C	7	22.5	24	77.5
T	11	27.5	29	72.5
Total	181	31.8%	388	68.2%

In about one-third of the institutions responding, elementary teachers complete a subject major outside of education; in two-thirds of the colleges they do not. The percentages do not vary considerably according to the type or size of institution. Presumably the major would be in a subject related to elementary teaching, such as English or mathematics, or be a broad fields major such as American studies. In addition, some colleges permit the prospective elementary teacher to substitute two subject minors for a subject major, as is indicated by the following data:

IN LIEU OF A SUBJECT MAJOR, ARE YOUR ELEMENTARY CANDIDATES PERMITTED TO SUBSTITUTE TWO OR MORE SUBJECT MINORS?				
	Yes	%	No	%
A	129	48.1%	139	51.9%
B	92	40.0	138	60.0
C	13	41.9	18	58.1
T	17	42.5	23	57.5
Total	251	44.1%	318	55.9%

An even higher percentage of elementary schools permit future elementary teachers to substitute two subject minors for a subject major than require the subject major. To some extent this increase may be caused by programs in which students major in education but are required to complete two minors in subject areas.

ARE STUDENTS PREPARING TO TEACH IN ELEMENTARY SCHOOL REQUIRED TO COMPLETE FRESHMAN ENGLISH?				
	Yes	%	No	%
A	267	99.7%	1	.3%
B	229	99.6	1	.4
C	31	100	0	0.
T	40	100	0	0.
Total	567	99.6%	2	.4%

---

[5] All percentage figures in this report refer to the percentage of the total number of institutions responding to the survey (n = 569).

Virtually all institutions require candidates to complete freshman English, a course which in most institutions concentrates on elementary principles of rhetoric and composition. In such courses, students compete with college students from all subject fields, nonacademic as well as academic. Normally the standards for *passing* such courses are established at the minimal levels of proficiency required for subsequent written work in the institution. In no sense does completion of such a course guarantee that students are prepared for teaching language and composition.

IN ADDITION TO FRESHMAN ENGLISH, HOW MANY SEMESTER CREDIT HOURS IN ENGLISH ARE REQUIRED OF STUDENTS PREPARING FOR ELEMENTARY TEACHING?

	0-6 semester hours			7-12 semester hours	
	No.	%		No.	%
A	148	55.2%	A	100	37.3%
B	124	53.9	B	90	39.1
C	13	41.9	C	14	45.2
T	16	40	T	19	47.5
Total	301	52.8%	Total	223	39.1%

	13-18 semester hours			More than 19 semester hours	
	No.	%		No.	%
A	16	6.0%	A	4	1.5%
B	11	4.8	B	5	2.2
C	4	12.9	C	0	0
T	5	12.5	T	0	0
Total	36	6.5%	Total	9	1.6%

Slightly more than half of the institutions report that prospective elementary teachers are *not* required to complete more than 6 semester hours in English, beyond the freshman level. This is the equivalent of requiring either one semester or one year's course in language or literature. In addition, 39.1 per cent of the schools report that students preparing for elementary teaching are required to complete 7 to 12 semester hours in English beyond the freshman level.

The mean requirements in terms of semester hours reported by colleges in each category are as follows:

	Mean No. Semester Hours	Range
A	7.1 hours	0 to 24 hours
B	8.1 hours	0 to 25 hours
C	8.9 hours	0 to 18 hours
T	8.0 hours	0 to 16 hours
Total	8.1 hours	

According to this survey, the mean national requirement is 8.1 semester hours in English beyond the freshman course, or the equivalent of more than two semesters of work. However, an analysis of the data indicates that in forty-one institutions, or about seven per cent of the total responding, students planning to become elementary teachers are not required to complete any work in English beyond the freshman level.

What Courses in Literature Are Required?

When asked to specify the courses in literature which students preparing for elementary teaching are required to complete, the institutions replied as follows:

	AMERICAN LITERATURE			ENGLISH LITERATURE	
	No.	%		No.	%
A	80	29.9%	A	78	29.1%
B	66	28.7	B	76	33.0
C	12	38.7	C	15	48.4
T	16	40.	T	9	22.5
Total	174	30.6%	Total	178	31.3%

	WORLD LITERATURE			MASTERPIECES OF LITERATURE	
	No.	%		No.	%
A	47	17.9%	A	16	6.0%
B	49	21.3	B	15	6.5
C	10	32.2	C	1	3.2
T	7	17.5	T	3	7.5
Total	113	20.0%	Total	35	6.1%

	INTRODUCTION TO LITERATURE		OTHER REQUIREMENTS		
	No.	%		No.	%
A	33	12.3%	A	32	11.7%
B	26	11.7	B	19	8.3
C	7	22.6	C	5	16.1
T	7	17.5	T	6	15.0
Total	73	12.8%	Total	62	10.9%

STUDENTS PERMITTED TO SELECT COURSE		
	No.	%
A	53	19.8%
B	46	40.0
C	3	9.9
T	6	15.0
Total	108	18.9%

Thus, in fewer than one-fifth of the colleges are elementary teachers permitted to elect the courses in literature that they are to complete. In most cases colleges require work in English literature (31.3%), in American literature (30.6%), or world literature (20.0%). The fact that fewer than a third of the programs provide for either American literature or English literature clearly indicates the need for national guidance to strengthen elementary programs. Because most elementary programs in the upper grades often include some study of Americana (folklore, legends, American humor, ballads), familiarity with American literature seems both desirable and necessary.

ARE STUDENTS PREPARING FOR ELEMENTARY TEACHING REQUIRED TO COMPLETE A COURSE IN THE HISTORY AND STRUCTURE OF THE ENGLISH LANGUAGE?				
	Yes	%	No	%
A	12	2.2%	257	97.8%
B	12	5.2	217	94.8
C	4	13.0	27	87.0
T	2	5.0	38	95.0
Total	30	5.3%	539	94.7%

Only 5.3 per cent of the colleges require students preparing for elementary teaching to complete a course on the English language. The over-

whelming majority do not. Nor do most colleges require future elementary teachers to study grammar and usage, as is indicated by the following data.

ARE STUDENTS PREPARING FOR ELEMENTARY TEACHING REQUIRED TO COMPLETE A COURSE IN GRAMMAR AND USAGE?

	Yes	%	No	%
A	92	34.3%	176	65.7%
B	87	37.8	143	62.2
C	17	54.8	14	45.2
T	23	57.5	17	42.5
Total	219	38.5%	350	61.5%

In more than three-fifths of the colleges, students prepared as elementary teachers are not required to complete work in grammar and usage. How teachers without language preparation can be expected to direct the study of American English is a matter for great concern. The teaching of the structure and the operation of language requires special knowledge which can be developed only through disciplined study. The data suggest that most elementary teachers are inadequately prepared to cope with such linguistic material.[6]

Other Special Requirements

The colleges were asked to indicate whether students preparing for elementary teaching were required to complete a course in any of the following important areas:

COMPOSITION BEYOND THE FRESHMAN LEVEL

	Yes	%	No	%
A	52	19.4%	216	80.6%
B	42	18.3	188	81.7
C	6	19.3	25	80.7
T	12	30.0	28	70.0
Total	112	19.7%	457	80.3%

---

[6] See discussion of the content of such courses on pages 61-69 and the data which reveal that few students receive good language training.

ORAL INTERPRETATION OF LITERATURE

	Yes	%	No	%
A	26	9.7%	243	90.3%
B	26	11.3	203	88.7
C	5	16.1	26	83.9
T	7	17.5	33	82.5
Total	64	11.2%	505	88.8%

SPEECH (other than oral interpretation)

	Yes	%	No	%
A	197	73.6%	71	26.4%
B	163	70.9	67	19.1
C	24	77.4	7	22.6
T	25	62.5	15	37.5
Total	409	71.9%	160	18.1%

Perhaps less necessary for all elementary teachers, but important for some, is specialized work in speech correction and creative dramatics. When asked if such courses are required, the colleges reported as follows:

SPEECH CORRECTION

	Yes	%	No	%
A	27	10.1%	241	89.9%
B	22	9.6	208	90.4
C	3	9.6	28	90.4
T	4	10.	36	90.
Total	56	9.8%	513	90.2%

CREATIVE DRAMATICS

	Yes	%	No	%
A	15	5.6%	253	94.4%
B	8	3.4	222	96.6
C	0	0.	31	100.0
T	2	5.0	38	95.0
Total	25	4.4%	544	95.6%

More than seventy per cent of the programs include a requirement in speech, the only one of these special offerings required of a majority of students preparing to teach elementary education. Only 19.7 per cent of the programs specify study in composition beyond the freshman level. Even fewer institutions require courses in the oral interpretation of literature (11.2%), speech correction (9.8%), or creative dramatics (4.4%). Some knowledge of these fields can be important to the elementary school teacher, even though all teachers may not be able to take work to an equal extent in every field. At present only a small percentage of teachers complete work in any one of these special subjects.

HOW MANY SEMESTER HOURS ARE ELEMENTARY TEACHERS REQUIRED TO COMPLETE IN PROFESSIONAL COURSES DEALING WITH THE METHODS OF TEACHING AND CONTENT OF READING AND THE LANGUAGE ARTS?

	0-5 semester hours		6-10 semester hours		Over 11 semester hours		Did not respond	
	No.	%	No.	%	No.	%	No.	%
A	186	69.4%	76	28.3%	4	1.5%	2	0.8%
B	161	70.0	48	20.9	7	3.0	14	6.1
C	19	61.3	7	22.6	4	12.9	1	3.2
T	25	62.5	12	30.	2	5.0	1	2.5
Total	391	68.7%	143	25.2%	17	3.0%	18	3.1%

If the preparation of the elementary teacher in language, composition, and literature is limited, his preparation in courses in professional education related to English teaching at the elementary level is also weak. More than two-thirds of the institutions report that no more than 5 semester hours are required in the methods of teaching and the content of reading and the language arts.

Coupled with the finding reported earlier that an average of 8.1 semester hours of English (beyond the freshman course) is required of such students, these data indicate that the average elementary program requires only a combined total of 12 or 13 semester hours of work in English and in the teaching of English at the elementary level. This median figure represents not more than *10* per cent of the 120 semester hours required for graduation in most four-year programs. As preparation to teach a subject that embraces two of the three R's, this requirement is surely insufficient.

IN WHAT SPECIAL AREAS OF PROFESSIONAL EDUCATION ARE STUDENTS REQUIRED TO COMPLETE A COURSE?

	Children's literature				Reading				Teaching language arts other than reading			
	Yes	%	No	%	Yes	%	No	%	Yes	%	No	%
A	204	76.1	64	23.9	214	80.0	54	20.0	173	64.5	95	35.5
B	161	70.0	69	30.	172	74.8	58	25.2	111	38.3	119	61.7
C	20	64.5	11	35.5	15	48.4	16	51.6	11	35.5	20	64.5
T	31	77.5	9	22.5	33	82.5	7	17.5	27	67.5	13	32.5
Total	416	73.1	153	26.9	434	76.3	135	23.7	322	56.6	247	43.4

Seventy-three per cent of the programs require a course in children's literature, 76.3 per cent require work in reading, and 56.6 per cent in the language arts other than reading. Since two-thirds of the elementary education students do not complete more than 5 semester hours in courses on the teaching of the language arts, some of the offerings must be combined or presented as one- or two-hour courses. The finding that only slightly more than half of the programs require work in the language arts is especially distressing in view of the limited preparation of these students in grammar, usage, and the structure of the English language.

Because questions arise concerning the relative emphasis within courses in children's literature, the institutions were asked to indicate in which department the course is offered. The replies were as follows:

	English		Education		Library Science	
A	100	37.3%	86	32.1%	25	9.3%
B	95	41.3	65	28.3	15	6.5
C	8	25.8	10	32.3	1	3.2
T	10	25.	19	47.5	2	5.0
Total	213	37.4%	180	33.4%	43	7.5%

The course in children's literature is offered in the department of English in over one-third of the responding schools and in the department of education in almost as many. Only 7.5 per cent of the schools offer the course in library science.

ARE STUDENTS PREPARING TO TEACH ELEMENTARY SUBJECTS REQUIRED TO COMPLETE A GENERAL COURSE IN ELEMENTARY SCHOOL METHODS?				
	Yes	%	No	%
A	173	64.5%	95	35.5%
B	111	41.4	119	58.6
C	11	35.5	20	64.5
T	27	67.5	13	32.5
Total	322	56.6%	247	43.4%

In more than half of the institutions a general methods course is required, although this practice seems to vary in different kinds of schools. In some colleges such a course is required in addition to the special courses on methods of teaching English in the elementary school.

HOW MUCH OF THE TIME IN THE GENERAL METHODS COURSE IS DEVOTED TO THE TEACHING OF READING AND THE OTHER LANGUAGE ARTS?				
Time devoted to reading				
	0-15%	16-25%	26-50%	over 51%
A	37	34	32	6
B	33	45	38	5
C	2	5	5	0
T	7	6	5	0
Total	79	90	80	11
Time devoted to language arts				
	0-15%	16-25%	26-50%	over 51%
A	42	39	33	2
B	30	52	36	2
C	5	3	1	1
T	3	8	3	1
Total	80	102	73	6
Time devoted to other problems				
	0-15%	16-25%	26-50%	over 51%
A	13	12	37	54
B	17	11	48	42
C	1	1	3	5
T	2	5	4	6
Total	33	29	92	107

The findings reveal that a considerable percentage of the work in general methods courses is related to the teaching of English, although emphasis in such courses is necessarily on subjects other than English.

Summary

Data from 569 institutions preparing students to teach in elementary schools reveal certain pronounced deficiencies in the preparation of the teachers in English. Although virtually all programs require students to complete freshman English, and usually speech, most require not more than two or three additional semesters of work in college English and not more than five semester hours in courses which deal with the teaching of reading, children's literature, and elementary language arts. Requirements in literature vary from school to school; not more than one-third of the institutions require American literature or English literature. A particular deficiency is to be noted in the failure of more than ninety per cent of the programs to provide for adequate study of the English language. Only a small percentage of the students take courses in the English language or English grammar and usage; only slightly more than half are even asked to take work in education which deals with content and methods of teaching the language arts. The need to strengthen the language preparation of elementary teachers is clearly as critical as the need to strengthen the language preparation of secondary teachers as is described in the next report.

THE ENGLISH LANGUAGE PREPARATION OF SECONDARY TEACHERS OF ENGLISH[7]

Highlights

Only a fourth of the colleges require a course in the history of the English language.

Only 17.4 per cent of the colleges require a course in Modern English grammar.

Fewer than 200 institutions are graduating teachers of English informed about modern language study.

Only 41 per cent of the colleges require prospective teachers of English to complete a course in advanced composition.

Only 51.5 per cent of the colleges require prospective teachers to complete a course in methods of teaching English.

[7] The material in this chapter is based on a study conducted by Harold B. Allen.

The Background

During the nineteenth century and the early years of the twentieth, linguistic science progressed and made available a vast number of new insights into the nature of English, a body of knowledge that was not only fresh and scientifically valid but also in direct contradiction to much of what was persistently being taught in the schools, in both England and the United States.

In 1921 Professor Henry Cecil Wyld acknowledged this discrepancy in a statement made during his inaugural lecture as professor of English philology at Oxford University: He said that although English "philology [i.e., linguistics] possesses a strange fascination for the man in the street, . . . almost everything he thinks and says about it is incredibly and hopelessly wrong. In no subject, probably, is the knowledge of the educated public at a lower ebb. The general ignorance concerning it is so profound that it is very difficult to persuade people that there really is a considerable mass of well-ascertained fact and a definite body of scientific doctrine on linguistic questions."[8]

Three years later in America Professor Leonard Bloomfield, speaking at the founding meeting of the Linguistic Society of America, declared: "Our schools are conducted by persons who, from professors of education down to teachers in the classroom, know nothing of the results of linguistic science, not even the relation of writing to speech, or of standard language to dialect. In short, they do not know what language is, and yet must teach it, and in consequence waste years of every child's life and reach a poor result."[9]

Important recommendations

Not long after Professor Bloomfield's address the feeling was so strong among a number of the country's leading English language specialists that, acting as an authorized committee of the National Council of Teachers of English, they drew up a momentous programmatic statement which was published in the Council's *English Journal* in December, 1928. This report pointed to the chasm between genuine language knowledge and the current language superstitions taught in the schools and sought a specific means of bringing about the gradual substitution of a scientific attitude for the eighteenth century assumptions then taught. The best means, the committee agreed, seemed to be the providing of proper training for the college and university students who were preparing them-

---

[8] Henry Cecil Wyld, *English Philology in English Universities* (Oxford: Clarendon Press, 1921), p. 10.
[9] Leonard Bloomfield, "Why a Linguistic Society?" *Language*, Vol. 1 (1925), p. 5.

selves to teach English. Accordingly, the report offered a description of the minimum essentials of linguistic knowledge for the prospective teacher and an outline of a course which would supply those essentials. The committee called for "adequate study of the historical development of English pronunciation, grammar, and vocabulary," but stated also that "a knowledge of the principles of general linguistics is of greater value to the teacher of English than a knowledge of the details of the history of the language."

With the purpose of ascertaining whether, after a period of several years, the committee's recommendations were being followed anywhere, in 1935 Harold B. Allen (then an instructor at the University of Michigan), sponsored by the NCTE, made a survey of the actual practices employed in providing linguistically sound English training for prospective teachers of English. The 373 returned questionnaires revealed a thoroughly unsatisfactory situation. Fewer than half of the responding colleges and universities offered any training in the English language. Most of the minimum training that was offered emphasized historical background or reviewed the condemned traditional grammar, sometimes both. Only a handful of institutions offered courses stressing the linguistic principles called for in the committee's report. The 1928 report actually had made almost no impact in seven years, despite its status as an official recommendation of the national organization concerned with the teaching of English in the schools. A number of the persons filling out the questionnaires expressed their individual regrets that inadequate staff, insufficient budget, lack of suitable textbooks, the pressure of the demand for traditional grammar from the uninformed and the unaware, and rigid certification requirements—all prevented their doing what they recognized as desirable. Only a few then saw hope in the immediate future.

Advances in language study

During the quarter century since that survey, spectacular advances have been made in the field of descriptive linguistics, particularly with respect to the analysis of English structure. These advances, linguists have pointed out, constitute a breakthrough comparable to those in physics and mathematics. The progress makes obsolete much of what was doctrinal in the discipline before 1930. Articles describing aspects of this revolution have appeared in the various journals of the National Council of Teachers of English and elsewhere. In successive national conventions of the Council and of its constituent group, the Conference on College Composition and Communication, much of the program has been devoted to these developments in English linguistics and their implications for teaching English language, grammar, composition, and literature in school and college. Furthermore, since 1954 the discoveries of linguistic research into English structure have been made available in two high school textbooks, at least three books for the college freshman course, and three for the undergraduate course in English structure. A useful collection of recent articles on "applied" linguistics has also appeared.

In the light of this increasing accessibility of sound linguistic information, it seemed pertinent to reassess currently the language preparation of the prospective teacher of English. To what extent had this preparation followed the recommendations of the 1928 committee? What acknowledgment had been made of the insistent demands of linguistic scholars that the schools reduce what had been termed the greatest cultural lag in any academic discipline? This reassessment, in the form of another survey undertaken under NCTE auspices by Professor Allen, provides a mass of data revealing the current situation in a significant proportion of colleges and universities.

Scope of the Survey

To give every eligible institution an opportunity to provide its own data, questionnaires were sent in April, 1960, to a nonselective list of 2,000 institutions offering work past the secondary school. Expedience dictated the choice of the time, which admittedly was less desirable than late October or early November. Even so, 545, or more than one-fourth, of the questionnaires had been returned by November 1, 1960. A number of these, totaling 171, were rejected as being from junior colleges, art schools, theological seminaries, exclusively technological institutions, and other schools offering no major work in English. The valid remaining responses, as of November 1, numbered 374, one more than in the 1935 survey and with equally wide geographical and institutional coverage.

The information sought by the questionnaire included:

Number of senior English majors preparing for secondary school teaching—both as of May, 1960, and as an annual average for the preceding five years.

Total credit hours required in English language, literature, and composition, for the nonteaching English major, the teaching English major, and the teaching English minor.

Undergraduate English language courses, and whether they are required.

Textbooks used in the English language courses.
Methods of conducting these courses.
Departments in which the courses are offered.
Principal changes in English language courses since 1950.
Likelihood of future changes.
Requirement of advanced composition.
Availability of an English methods course, and its requirement status.
Type and amount of credit offered by the methods course in English.
Content of the methods course with respect to ways of teaching traditional grammar, applications of modern structural linguistics, usage, and composition.
In addition, supplementary information if the questionnaire did not adequately represent the local situation.

Selected Significant Data from the Survey

Returns were initially classified in two groups—those from liberal arts colleges and those from teachers colleges; those in the former group were then subdivided according to the size of the full time student body. Institutions having more than 1000 full time students (according to the 1960 World Almanac table) were classed in the A group; between 301 and 1000 in the B group; fewer than 301 in the C group. The teachers colleges are classed under T. This same classification was used in 1935. Although many institutions replying in 1935 also replied in 1960, the two groups of colleges differ somewhat. Nevertheless, the size of the sample in each survey—about a fourth of the total eligible population—is such as to imply high reliability. The 1960 total valid response will henceforth be identified simply as R, with AR, BR, CR, and TR representing the total responses in the various categories.

DISTRIBUTION OF RESPONSES

		1935	1960
Liberal arts colleges	A	53	137
	B	153	180
	C	97	31
		303	348
Teachers colleges	T	70	26
		373	374

The shift in the distribution of responses reflects two well-known facts. One is the larger college enrollment today, with consequent shifting of some colleges from the C to B category, and others from the B to A category. The other is the transformation of many former "normal schools" and "teachers colleges" to "state colleges" offering work in the liberal arts along with work in professional education; hence the decline in the number classed in the T group.

SENIORS PREPARING TO TEACH HIGH SCHOOL ENGLISH

Yearly average, 1955-1960

	Total	Institutions	Ave. per inst.	1930-35 ave.
A	2546	111	23.	35
B	1248.4	167	7.4	14
C	83.7	23	3.7	7
T	420	22	19.	16
	4298.1	323	13.3	16

1959-1960 seniors

	Total	Institutions	Ave. per inst.	
A	2984	114	26.5	
B	1389	169	8.2	
C	166	24	7.	
T	464	23	19.5	
	5003	330	15.2	

In June, 1960, more college seniors were graduated as prospective teachers of high school English than had been graduated, on the average, during each year of the preceding five-year period. Yet the actual average increase per institution is only 1.9 (from 13.5 to 15.4), not enough to keep pace with the normally increasing demands for teachers of English. The institutional average for the past year, 1959-60, actually is less than it was during the period from 1930-35, despite the great increase in the country's population and in the school population during the past twenty-five years. In short, there are not enough college students being prepared to teach English in the schools; and unless there is a change in the rate of population growth with a corresponding increase in the number of prospective teachers, the disparity will grow greater each year.

More students needed

Minimal English credit requirements

Semester (or equivalent) credits in English (including literature and composition but excluding freshman English) required of candidates for high school teaching with English major:

	24 or less	25 to 30	31 or more	Total
A	47	54	22	123
B	64	70	20	154
C	9	12	4	25
T	8	4	8	20
Total	128 39.3%	140 43.5%	54 16.6%	322 100%
	34% of R	37.4% of R	14.4% of R	86.5% of R

Semester credits in English required of candidates with an English minor:

	17 or less	18 or more	Total
A	28	71	99
B	50	73	123
C	4	11	15
T	7	9	16
Total	89 35%	164 65%	253 100%
	23.8% of R	44% of R	67% of R

The above tables indicate that of those college seniors who in June, 1960, intended to teach high school English, those in 40 per cent of the institutions providing answers for this item were required to have no more than 24 semester hour credits in English. Four colleges, indeed, required only 18 such credits for the major.

Furthermore, those seniors who took only an English minor but who, as data presented earlier show,[10] are quite likely to turn up as authorities in the English classroom, were still less well prepared with subject-content in the field. In 89 institutions such possible future teachers of English needed to obtain fewer than 18 semester credits. In three colleges they could get by with only 10 semester credits, in five with only 9, and in one institution 6 credits in English were deemed sufficient to qualify a student to teach high school English if the opportunity came to him.

---

[10] See pages 35-36.

AVAILABILITY OF ENGLISH LANGUAGE COURSES

	No.	Inst. offering course Pct.	'35 pct.	Requiring it of English majors No.	Pct.	'35 pct.	Requiring it of English minors No.	Pct.
Old English								
A	36	26	61	3	2.2	4	0	0
B	5	2.8	33	0	0	7	0	0
C	1	3.2	7	0	0	6	0	0
T	1	4	16	0	0	6	0	0
Total	43	11.7	24	3	.8	6	0	0
Hist. of Eng. Lang.								
A	105	77	67	47	35	13	22	15
B	86	47.5	31	42	23	14	18	10
C	8	26	28	5	16	13	1	3.2
T	17	65	39	1	3.8	17	6	23
Total	216	58	40	95	25.3	14	47	12.5
Phonetics								
A	31	22.7	32	7	5.1	0	6	4.4
B	20	11.1	19	6	3.3	2	2	1.1
C	1	3.2	10	0	0	2	0	0
T	8	31	9	2	7.7	1	1	3.8
Total	60	16	17	15	4.	2	9	2.4
American English								
A	23	16.8		2	1.46		2	1.46
B	3	1.7		4	2.2		4	2.2
C	3	9.7		1	3.2		1	3.2
T	4	15.4		2	7.7		2	7.7
Total	33	8.8		9	2.4		9	2.4
Formal Grammar Review								
A	23	16.8		18	3.2		10	7.3
B	27	15		17	9.5		10	5.5
C	4	13		4	13		3	9.7
T	6	23		3	11.5		0	0
Total	60	16		42	11.2		23	6.1

Modern English Grammar								
A	57	41.6	36	31	22.6	4	17	12.5
B	39	21.6	31	28	15.5	9	12	6.7
C	3	9.7	22	3	9.7	7	0	0
T	6	23	50	3	11.2	23	2	7.7
Total	105	28	33	65	17.4	10	31	8.3
Grammar and Usage								
A	18	13		6	4.4		4	2.9
B	19	9.5		9	5.2		8	4.4
C	2	6.5		1	3.2		0	0
T	1	3.8		1	3.8		0	0
Total	40	10.7		17	4.5		12	3.2

The English language content offered in undergraduate courses can be classified under the six headings used in the questionnaire and repeated in the preceding tables. These six kinds are in a rough sequence according to the predicted specificity of the content. The first, listed as Old English and sometimes called Anglo-Saxon, is a well-standardized course with a sharply limited range of content and quite specific objectives. At the other extreme would be a course dealing with grammar and usage, which could be almost anything the instructor would like to make of it.

Several significant generalizations can be drawn from the foregoing data. During the past twenty-five years, for example, there has been a noticeable decline in the number of institutions offering Old English as an undergraduate course and requiring it of prospective teachers. Contrasting with this trend, but not quite balancing it, is an increase in the number of institutions offering the history of the language, Modern English grammar, and phonetics. But this trend is still not quite a significant one, since even in 1960 only a fourth of the responding colleges require the history of the language, and only 17 per cent require a course that could be classed as Modern English grammar.

Limited offerings in language courses

Indeed, the present situation does not offer strong evidence of general acceptance of the long-standing report of the National Council of Teachers of English. Only three of the 374 responding institutions (R) require the would-be English teacher to have a course in Old English; only 95, about one-fourth, require the history of the English language;

only 15, or 4 per cent, require a course in phonetics; only 9, or 2.4 per cent, require a course in American English; and only 17, or 4.5 per cent, require a course in which some relationship between grammar and usage is stressed. Forty-two, or 11.2 per cent, require the prospective teacher to take a course which simply reviews the fundamentals of the traditional outmoded grammatical analysis and terminology. Nor does the evidence suggest that many students are required to pursue these separate studies in any combination course on the English language.

Clearly, even if it could be assumed that the course in grammar and usage and that in Modern English grammar reflect in measurable degree the linguistic advances of the past quarter century, only a minority of the English majors are required to take such courses. But that assumption itself is unwarranted. Many of the textbooks reported as being used in these two courses are textbooks entirely in the outmoded tradition. Apparently the rubric, "Modern English grammar," despite the implications of the covering letter, was interpreted by some college instructors as referring to a systematic study of the old-fashioned grammatical apparatus with not so much as a hint of the existence of linguistic science and applications in English language studies. In effect, then, many of the institutions included in this category should more accurately be tallied under the heading, "Review of Formal Grammar," a correspondingly smaller number considered as actually providing the prospective teacher with understanding of the modern structural principles of linguistic analysis. Upon the basis of the use of textbooks with actual linguistic content, it would seem that not more than 69 of the 374 responding institutions make linguistic information available in the course; in reality, the number is less than that, perhaps about fifty, or approximately fifteen per cent, since in some colleges more than one of the listed books are used in a single course.

Informed majors are a minority

Since the 374 responding institutions constitute about one-fourth of the total number of four-year liberal arts colleges and departments in the country, extrapolation of this maximum figure for the examined group would probably justify a rough estimate that at the most fewer than 200 institutions in the United States are currently graduating prospective teachers of English whose preparation includes even rudimentary attention to the modern objective approach to their language through structural linguistics.

One-fourth of the institutions offer needed courses

REQUIREMENT OF ADVANCED COMPOSITION						
	Regular English major		Teaching major		Teaching minor	
A	54	39%	66	46%	43	31.2%
B	34	18.8	64	35	39	21.6
C	12	39	14	45	8	26
T	17	65	10	38.5	10	38.5
Total	117	31%	154	41%	100	26.8%

About one-third of the respondents (R) require their English majors to have at least one course in advanced composition beyond that usually found in the freshman year. Only a slightly higher proportion, 41 per cent, require it of the majors who are intending to teach; and only 26 per cent require it of the English minors. Similar results were also found in a 1960 survey of 1247 colleges by the Commission on English of the College Entrance Examination Board which reported that "one third of the institutions do not offer such courses even on an elective basis."[11]

Advanced composition not always offered

The fact that about three out of five English majors and three out of four English minors are not required to complete advanced work in composition is especially disturbing in view of the vital necessity for improving present programs for teaching composition. James B. Conant calls for fifty per cent of high school English courses to be devoted to the teaching of composition.[12] The National Association of Secondary-School Principals emphasizes that "during each school semester, provision must be made to teach writing systematically, sequentially, and continuously."[13] The Commission on English of the College Entrance Examination Board flatly states, "Composition should be neither infrequent nor incidental. It should be part of each week's work and should be intimately connected with the other parts of that work."[14] For many years similar recommendations have been published by the Commission on the Curriculum of the National Council of Teachers of English, a group which has long worked for greater emphasis on the teaching of composition. Yet how are teachers to help students understand basic principles of logic and rhetoric to which they themselves have scarcely been introduced?

[11]"Report on College Courses in Composition," Commission on English of College Entrance Examination Board, 183 Commonwealth Avenue, Boston 16, Massachusetts, 1960 (unpublished).
[12]James B. Conant, *The American High School Today* (New York: McGraw-Hill, 1960), pp. 50-51.
[13]*English Language Arts in the Comprehensive Secondary School*, National Association of Secondary-School Principals (Washington: National Education Association, 1960), p. 6.
[14]"Preparation in English for College-Bound Students," Commission on English of the College Entrance Examination Board, 1960, p. 6.

THE ENGLISH METHODS COURSE

English methods course offered?	Yes		No		No response		Total	
A	117	85%	18	13.2%	2	4.5%	137	AR
B	120	66.5	51	28	9	5	180	BR
C	19	58	11	35.2	1	3.2	31	CR
T	25	96	1	3.8	0	0	26	TR
Total	281	75%	81	21.6%	12	2.7%	374	R

Required of English majors?								
A	78	52%	38	27.8%	21	15.3%	137	AR
B	79	44	42	23.2	59	33	180	BR
C	12	38	6	19.3	13	42	31	CR
T	24	92	0	0	2	7.7	26	TR
Total	193	51.5%	86	23%	95	25.1%	374	R

Required of English minors?								
A	40	29%	62	45%	35	25.6%	137	AR
B	28	15.5	72	40	80	44.5	180	BR
C	2	6.5	13	42	16	51.5	31	CR
T	8	30.6	10	38.5	8	31	26	TR
Total	78	20.8%	157	42%	139	37%	374	R

Although certification for secondary teaching normally requires meeting a state provision that insists upon credit for a methods course, such a course may often include students with majors in diverse fields and hence of necessity be quite general. In the smaller colleges with a relatively small number of seniors planning to teach, this course is perforce one which ignores the specific subject areas. Although the instructor in such a course may sometimes give individual assignments in the student's special field, little detailed attention can be directed to the manifold and important problems of teaching literature, grammar, and composition.

The preceding tables reveal that only 75 per cent of the respondents (R) offer specific work in the methods of teaching English in the secondary school. As might be expected, nearly complete coverage is found in the teachers colleges and the most inadequate in the smaller liberal arts colleges. But even where offered, this course is not always required of the English major. Only 51.5 per cent of R make this a requirement. Only 20.8 per cent of R require it of the teaching candidate with an English minor.

TIME SPENT IN THE METHODS COURSE UPON METHODS OF TEACHING FORMAL GRAMMAR:

	None		Little		1-6 hrs.		7-12 hrs.		12+ hrs.		No response	
A	26	19%	7	5.1%	25	18%	30	22%	8	5.8%	41	30%
B	9	5	9	5	24	13.3	38	21	16	8.9	84	46.5
C	3	9.7	1	3.2	6	19.3	3	9.7	2	6.5	16	51.5
T	3	11.5	0	0	3	11.5	5	19	4	15.4	11	42
Tot.	41	11%	17	4.5%	58	15.5%	76	20.4%	30	8%	152	40.5%

75 — 20%
106 — 28.4%
181 — 48.4%

TIME SPENT IN THE METHODS COURSE UPON METHODS OF TEACHING ENGLISH USAGE:

	None		Little		1-6 hrs.		7-12 hrs.		12+ hrs.		No response	
A	24	17.5%	9	6.5%	29	21%	21	15.4%	6	4.3%	48	35%
B	7	3.9	7	3.9	27	15	30	16.7	18	10	91	50
C	2	6.5	2	6.5	2	6.5	2	6.5	2	6.5	21	68
T	1	3.8	0	0	4	15.5	7	27	1	3.8	13	50
Tot.	34	9.1%	18	4.8%	62	16.5%	60	16%	27	7.2%	173	46%

80 — 21.3%
87 — 23.2%
167 — 44.5%

In more than half of R, the controlling opinion seems to be that traditional formal grammar can be sufficiently well taught by the beginning teacher without any instruction in grammar methods. Only 181 institutions, 48.4 per cent of R, report that any such instruction is provided; only 106 of these, or 28.4 per cent of R, spend more than two weeks upon how to teach grammar.

A similar situation appears with respect to helping the prospective teacher teach matters of usage. Although some attention to the teaching of usage is in itself no guarantee that the attitude toward usage is scientifically valid, even the recognition of usage as important may very likely be looked upon as a step in the right direction. But again more than one-half of R do not report any such instruction at all. By and large the prospective teacher is more likely left with the nonobjective prejudices and notions prevalent in the usual freshman composition class. Only 167, or 44.5 per cent, seem to pay attention at all to the problems of teaching usage; only about half of this number, or 23 per cent of R, spend more than a minimum of six hours upon this basic responsibility in teaching English.

Fewer than half study English usage

DOES THE METHODS COURSE DEVOTE ANY TIME TO STRUCTURAL LINGUISTICS?						
	Yes		Very little		No	
A	44	32%	12	8.8%	54	39.3%
B	35	19.4	16	8.9	50	27.7
C	3	9.6	1	3.2	15	48
T	6	23	13	50	12	46
Total	88	23.5%	42	11.2%	131	35%

It has already been observed that 18 per cent of the responding institutions require the prospective English teacher to have a course in Modern English grammar, and that often this heading refers to content drawn from contemporary linguistic data. In most of these institutions, as well apparently as in others not having such an English language course available, the methods course offers help in making some application of linguistics to the high school classroom. But usually, even then, the help is meager and the time spent is small. Of the 130 institutions, 35 per cent of R, claiming to offer such help, 42, or 11.2 per cent, frankly admit that the time spent is "very little," often amounting to no more than a day or two spent in summary indication of the existence of linguistics and of its recent impact upon the teaching of English. That is, a maximum of 88 institutions, or less than 24 per cent of the total responding, lay even a part of the foundation which the prospective teacher must stand on if he is to apply new principles of language study in the classroom.

Methods course offers little help

DOES THE METHODS COURSE DEVOTE ATTENTION TO METHODS IN TEACHING COMPOSITION?						
	Yes		No		?	
A	98	65%	9	6.5%	7	5.1%
B	100	55	6	3.3	1	.55
C	13	42	2	6.5	0	0
T	21	81	3	11.5	0	0
Total	232	62.5%	20	5.35%	8	2.12%

TIME ALLOTTED TO METHODS OF TEACHING COMPOSITION						
	Less than 3 weeks		3-5 weeks		More than 5 weeks	
A	23	16.8%	50	36.3%	13	9.5%
B	23	12.7	53	29.2	5	2.8
C	8	26	8	26	1	3.2
T	0	0	14	54	3	11.5
Total	54	14.3%	125	33%	22	5.9%

The methods course does slightly better for composition than for grammar and usage. Even so, more than a third of such courses frankly ignore problems in the teaching of composition, important as that subject is in the high school curriculum and in the needs of high school students. Most of the institutions, 125 of the 201, which do consider composition problems spend between three to five weeks upon them. Fifty-four, or about one-fourth, apparently consider less than that small time adequate.

Summary

This survey makes clear that the linguistic preparation of the prospective English teachers in the United States is grievously deficient. Whatever their preparation in other areas, it is seriously inadequate with respect to their concern with the teaching of the nature and use of the English language, that is, with respect to grammar, usage, and composition. Professor Bloomfield's description of the state of affairs in 1924, quoted at the beginning of this section, would need only slight modification to be equally accurate today.

New opportunities for teachers

The few institutions offering work based on the traditional eighteenth century Latinate grammar may hardly be said to contribute anything constructive. Since the days when, for want of a better available content, there were reasonable arguments for such grammar, a revolution in linguistic science has occurred. The advances in philology during the nineteenth century have been followed by a total reorientation of the field of linguistic study in the second quarter of the twentieth century. This reorientation, appearing in what is termed structural linguistics, has now opened to teachers of English a door to new insights and new learning. It offers materials for a realistic and scientifically sound methodology in developing the ability to use the language with increasing skill and power. Already some of its methods and materials have been successfully used in teaching English as a foreign language, especially in the English programs our country and its foundations have sponsored and aided abroad. But this survey reveals that, despite the urgent need and the public demand for improvement in high school teaching, the colleges and universities have been slow to adjust to the linguistic revolution. Only a small proportion of them require prospective teachers to take a course with modern linguistic content; indeed, most do not offer such a course and evince no interest in making a change. Only a small proportion offer an English methods in which the existence of a valid linguistic grammar is even recognized, much less dealt with in detail.

There seems to be almost no recognition of the discovery of Professor Charles C. Fries in 1940 that a quantitative analysis of English sentences points to the need for stress upon syntax, not upon grammar as such, as the means to develop a mature style; for modern linguistics is the door to the understanding of English syntax.

In short, most of the English majors who were graduated in June, 1960, and are now teaching in high school are simply not equipped either to deal with problems of teaching the language and composition or to keep up with current developments in the application of linguistics to the teaching of English. Unhappily, what is true of the class of 1960 is no less true of previous classes and hence of the great body of teachers now in English classrooms; and it likely will be true of future graduating classes for some time unless the normally slow sequence of events can be modified.

Most teachers of English lack preparation in language

In the fields of science and mathematics, where the cultural lag was less acute, the spectacular appearance of Sputnik provided the impetus for re-examination and for such developments as the re-education of leading high school science teachers. In English the disparity between what specialists and research scholars know and what the schools teach is even greater than it was in science, but no dramatic orbiting of a linguistic satellite draws public attention to this disparity.

THE PREPARATION IN LITERATURE OF SECONDARY TEACHERS OF ENGLISH

Highlights

More than fifty per cent of the colleges require future high school teachers who major in English to complete 18 to 24 semester hours in literature.

More than two-thirds of the colleges require courses in English literature, American literature, and Shakespeare; only one-third require work in world literature.

Only one-fifth of the programs specify the need for a course in contemporary literature or in literary criticism or critical analysis.

Few institutions provide for the study of the literature written for adolescents.

More time is spent in methods courses on the teaching of literature than on the teaching of grammar and the teaching of composition combined.

Scope of the Survey

During the spring of 1960, a survey of the preparation of teachers of English in language (reported earlier in this section) revealed startling deficiencies in college programs for undergraduates preparing to teach English. A question immediately arose concerning the adequacy of preparation in literature for prospective teachers of English. To obtain information on the preparation in literature of prospective teachers of secondary English, questionnaires were sent in late September, 1960, to a nonselective list of 2,000 institutions offering work beyond the high school level. These were the same institutions that earlier had received questionnaires on the language preparation of teachers. Within ninety days, 831 questionnaires, or 41.5 per cent, had been returned. Three hundred and seventy-seven of the replies were from schools which do not prepare teachers of high school English. The remaining responses totaled 454 and represent great institutional and regional variation. Questions asked in the survey included:

The number of credit hours in literature required of students preparing to teach English with a major in English.

The extent to which work in the following areas is required of students preparing to teach with a major in English: Shakespeare, English literature, American literature, world literature, masterpieces of literature, Chaucer or Middle English literature, period courses in seventeenth, eighteenth, nineteenth century literature, contemporary literature.

Information on whether students are required to take a course in literary criticism or critical analysis.

Information on whether students are required to take a course dealing with a literary genre or genres, and, if so, the areas in which students are required to complete work, e.g., poetry, fiction, nonfiction, drama.

Information on whether students are required to complete a course in literature for children or adolescents and, if so, the department in which the course is offered, e.g., English, education, library science.

Information on whether students are required to take a course in methods of teaching English and, in such courses, the number of hours devoted to the study of literature.

Selected Data from the Survey

An attempt was made to classify returns in categories paralleling those in the study on the English language preparation of teachers. Returns were first divided into those from the liberal arts colleges and universities and those from teachers colleges; those in the former group were subdivided into categories based on the size of each institution. Institutions having more than 1000 full time students (according to the 1960 World Almanac) are classed in the A group; between 301 and 1000, in the B group; fewer than 301, in the C group. Teachers colleges are classified under T. In the report which follows, the total group responding is referred to as R.

DISTRIBUTION OF RESPONSES

Liberal Arts Colleges	A	239
Liberal Arts Colleges	B	184
Liberal Arts Colleges	C	20
		443
Teachers Colleges	T	11
Total institutions		454

A slightly greater percentage of large liberal arts colleges responded to this survey than to the one dealing with the English language preparation of teachers conducted five months earlier.[15] A smaller number of teachers colleges responded. However, both surveys indicate clearly that present high school teachers with a major in English are prepared mainly in liberal arts colleges. Ninety-three per cent of the responses in the spring survey came from liberal arts colleges as contrasted with ninety-eight per cent of the responses on this survey. These high percentages reflect the transformation of the teachers colleges and normal schools to liberal arts centers.

Semester Credit Hours in Literature Required of Students with an English Major

The semester credit hours in literature required of students who plan to teach high school English with a major in English (excluding freshman English):

	Below 18	18-24	25-30	31 or more	Total R
A	15	127	67	30	239
B	7	96	56	25	184
C	0	12	5	3	20
T	1	7	3	0	11
Total	23	242	131	58	454
	5.1%	53.3%	28.8%	12.8%	

[15] See page 64.

The findings indicate that the majority of students who are preparing to teach in high school with a major in English are required to complete no less than 24 hours in literature. Twenty-four semester credits is the equivalent of one three-hour course per semester. Forty-one per cent require more than the amount. Only 5.1 per cent of the institutions require fewer than 18 semester credits; however in 23 colleges, students may get by with less than 6 semesters of literary study. On the other hand 58 institutions, or 12.8 per cent of those responding, require students to complete more than 31 or more semester hours in literature.

Requirements in Specific Courses

The following tables indicate the extent to which students preparing to teach English in the high school with a major in English are required to complete specific courses.

ENGLISH LITERATURE (survey, major authors, major works)		
	No.	% of responses[16]
A	203	85.2%
B	163	88.6
C	18	90.0
T	10	90.9
Total	394	86.8%

AMERICAN LITERATURE (survey, major authors, major works)		
	No.	% of responses
A	192	80.3%
B	162	88.0
C	15	75.0
T	11	100.0
Total	380	83.7%

SHAKESPEARE		
	No.	% of responses
A	172	72.0%
B	139	75.6
C	13	65.0
T	7	63.6
Total	331	72.9%

[16] All percentages in this section indicate the percentage of the total number of institutions responding to the questionnaire (n = 454).

WORLD LITERATURE (survey, major authors, major works)

	No.	% of responses
A	66	27.6%
B	85	46.2
C	14	70.0
T	3	27.2
Total	168	37.0%

MASTERPIECES OF LITERATURE

	No.	% of responses
A	20	8.4%
B	24	13.0
C	1	5.0
T	1	9.1
Total	46	10.1%

CHAUCER OR MIDDLE ENGLISH LITERATURE

	No.	% of responses
A	80	33.5%
B	55	30.0
C	11	55.0
T	0	0.0
Total	146	32.2%

SEVENTEENTH CENTURY (survey or one course)

	No.	% of responses
A	48	20.1%
B	43	23.4
C	3	15.
T	2	18.2
Total	96	21.1%

EIGHTEENTH CENTURY (survey or one course)

	No.	% of responses
A	45	18.8%
B	42	22.8
C	6	30.0
T	0	0.0
Total	93	20.5%

NINETEENTH CENTURY (survey or one course)		
	No.	% of responses
A	60	25.3%
B	58	31.5
C	8	40.
T	0	0.0
Total	126	28.0%

CONTEMPORARY LITERATURE		
	No.	% of responses
A	43	18.0%
B	41	22.3
C	9	45.
T	3	27.3
Total	96	21.1%

Comment: The data reveal that requirements in literature for students planning to teach high school with a major in English are far more specific than the requirements in language.[17] Even so, certain deficiencies are apparent. About 85 per cent of the colleges require survey courses in English literature or American literature (15 per cent do not); only 72.9 per cent require course work in Shakespeare. These requirements are maintained in more than two-thirds of the colleges. Most specialists would agree that some work in these areas is vital and should be required of all. Beyond these three requirements, little agreement is apparent, as is indicated by the following rank order of the frequency in which courses in literature are required.

RANK ORDER OF FREQUENCY OF REQUIRED COURSES IN LITERATURE		
Rank	Course	% of colleges responding
1	English Literature (survey)	86.8%
2	American Literature (survey)	83.7
3	Shakespeare	72.9
4	World Literature (survey)	37.0
5	Chaucer or Middle English Literature	32.2
6	Nineteenth Century	28.0
7.5	Seventeenth Century	21.1
7.5	Contemporary Literature	21.1
9	Eighteenth Century	20.5
10	Masterpieces of Literature	10.1

---

[17] See pages 69-74.

World literature needed

Only a limited number of schools require study of world literature and contemporary literature, perhaps the most apparent weaknesses in existing programs of preparation. Only slightly more than one-third of the colleges require world literature and only one-fifth contemporary literature. Both are areas in which secondary schools provide many offerings. Obviously college programs cannot provide course work in every aspect of literature conceivably needed at some time by the teacher. More important than any accumulation of course credits is the approach to literature that the student learns. Still a teacher cannot teach content with which he remains unfamiliar, nor can he have an adequate basis for selecting literature to be taught in the schools unless he has some understanding of selections available. One can only hope that those English majors who are not required to complete such courses are strongly advised to take them. Some colleges may expect students to pass special examinations or to demonstrate otherwise the competences and understandings desired.

The increasing emphasis on world literature in the nation's schools makes highly desirable some introduction to this content. The difficulty of much contemporary literature poses special problems for the teacher, as does his problem of selecting works to be taught from literature which has not yet stood the test of time. Preparation in contemporary literature seems almost a necessity. While regrettable, the few requirements for period courses are of less concern, since students will necessarily be introduced to many of the important writings of each age during the survey courses.

ARE STUDENTS PREPARING TO TEACH IN HIGH SCHOOL WITH A MAJOR IN ENGLISH REQUIRED TO TAKE A COURSE IN LITERARY CRITICISM OR IN THE CRITICAL ANALYSIS OF LITERATURE?

	Yes	%	No	%
A	62	25.9%	177	71.1%
B	56	30.4	128	69.6
C	11	55.	9	45.
T	3	27.3	8	72.7
Total	132	29.1%	322	70.9%

More help in criticism needed

During the past twenty years, approaches in literary criticism and in methods of teaching literature have shifted perceptibly. In teaching, much less emphasis is placed on the historical approach, much more on critical analysis. To find that only 29.1 per cent of students planning to teach in high school with a major in English are required to complete a course in literary criticism or in the critical analysis of literature is disconcerting, especially since it seems unlikely that students educated only in broad historical survey courses can be well prepared for the newer approaches.

For several years most college instructors have recommended less emphasis on the chronological survey of literature, more on an intensive study of a few literary pieces.[18] Teachers who themselves are unable to apply various approaches to analyzing literature can scarcely be expected to be able to offer their students adequate help.

ARE STUDENTS PREPARING TO TEACH WITH A MAJOR IN ENGLISH REQUIRED TO TAKE A COURSE IN A LITERARY GENRE OR GENRES?

	Yes	%	No	%
A	87	36.4%	152	63.6%
B	74	40.2	110	59.8
C	10	50.	10	50.
T	5	45.8	6	54.5
Total	176	38.8%	278	61.2%

Comment: Only slightly more than one-third of the colleges require students who plan to teach in high school with an English major to take a course in a literary genre. Such courses offer an appropriate setting for providing instruction in critical analysis, yet the infrequency of the requirement suggests that most teachers do not complete such work.

Those colleges maintaining the requirement report that the following courses in literary genres are required:

	POETRY	
	Schools responding	% of responses
A	67	28.0%
B	49	21.2
C	8	40.
T	4	36.3
Total	128	28.2%

---

[18]Cf. James J. Lynch, "College Support for High School English Teachers: The California Plan," *College English*, XXI (November, 1959), pp. 73-80.

FICTION (novel, short story)

	No.	% of responses
A	56	23.4%
B	41	22.3
C	7	35.
T	3	27.2
Total	107	23.5%

NONFICTION (biography, essay)

	No.	% of responses
A	18	7.5%
B	19	10.3
C	4	20.
T	2	18.2
Total	43	9.5%

DRAMA

	No.	% of responses
A	44	18.4%
B	43	23.3
C	9	45.
T	3	27.2
Total	99	21.8%

Of the genre courses required, the most frequently mentioned is the course in poetry. Slightly more than 28 per cent of the total respondents require students planning to teach English to complete such a course; 21.8 per cent require a course in drama. Some colleges ask students to complete one or two genre courses but leave the choice to the student. Only 9.5 per cent require a course in nonfiction (essays, biography). This finding is not surprising in view of the limited interest in expository writing and advanced composition revealed in the survey of the English language preparation of teachers. Although a study of the literary essay and other nonfiction writing is in no way a satisfactory substitute for a course in advanced composition, those students who do study the forms of nonfiction inevitably learn something about logic and rhetorical principle which they can apply in teaching composition. Unfortunately, the number of students who are apparently required to complete such study is small and offers little hope that many future teachers are learning about principles of rhetoric and logic in this way.

ARE STUDENTS PREPARING TO TEACH WITH A MAJOR IN ENGLISH REQUIRED TO COMPLETE A COURSE IN LITERATURE FOR CHILDREN OR ADOLESCENTS?				
	Yes	%	No	%
A	38	15.9%	201	84.1%
B	29	15.7	155	84.3
C	4	20.	16	80.
T	1	9.1	10	90.1
Total	72	15.9%	382	84.1%

The standard of preparation for teachers of English presented earlier in this report calls for teachers to be informed about the literature that they teach. Especially between grades 7 and 10, high school teachers teach many books especially written for children and adolescents, both classics such as *The Adventures of Tom Sawyer*, *Bambi*, and *Treasure Island* and good recent books like *Caddie Woodlawn*, *Johnny Tremain*, and *On to Oregon*. Conventional courses in literature pay little attention to such selections, yet only 15.9 per cent of schools require students preparing to teach English in high school to complete a course in literature for children and adolescents.

Where such courses are required, colleges indicated the departments in which the course is offered. In 31 schools (6.8% of the 454 institutions), the required course in literature for children or adolescents is offered by the English department. In 38 colleges (8.3% of those responding), it is offered in education. In 12 schools (2.6%), it is a library science course. Some schools reported the course as offered by more than one department. The really significant finding, however, is that courses of this type are required at only 15.9 per cent of the institutions.

REQUIREMENT IN METHODS OF TEACHING

ARE STUDENTS PLANNING TO TEACH WITH A MAJOR IN ENGLISH REQUIRED TO TAKE A COURSE IN METHODS OF TEACHING ENGLISH?				
	Yes	%	No	%
A	187	78.2%	52	21.8%
B	123	66.8	61	33.2
C	15	75.	5	25.
T	9	81.8	2	18.2
Total	334	73.6%	120	26.4%

According to this survey, 73.6 per cent of colleges require major students planning to teach English in high school to take a course in methods of teaching English; 26.4 per cent do not. Students who are not required to take a course in methods of teaching English presumably complete a general methods course dealing with general principles of teaching rather than with methods of teaching the subject. The discrepancy between this finding and that reported in the survey of English language preparation should be noted.[19] Possibly the discrepancy is created by the failure of this question as here worded to discriminate between a course that is offered and one that is required. The 73.6 per cent "Yes" total corresponds closely to the 75 per cent of the colleges on the earlier study that indicated "offering" such a course. In any event, far too few of the colleges require such work even of majors in English. A much smaller percentage of the minors (and non-minors), those with the least preparation in English, are likely to have support from an English methods course. Teachers of English have repeatedly indicated that a methods course which is taught by a competent instructor is a valuable part of their preparation.[20] If teachers complete only a course in general methods of teaching or no course at all, they have little opportunity to develop vital understandings about the language development of young people, the psychology of subject matter pertaining to English, and what is known from research and experience about the teaching of literature, language, and composition.

Many lack methods of teaching English

WHEN A METHODS COURSE IS OFFERED, HOW MUCH TIME IS DEVOTED IN THIS COURSE TO STUDYING METHODS OF TEACHING LITERATURE?

	0 to 25 hours		25 to 36		36 to 50		over 50		no answer	
A	31	13.0%	34	14.2%	84	35.1%	20	8.4%	70	29.3%
B	20	10.9	26	14.1	49	26.6	21	11.4	68	37.0
C	3	15.	2	10.	9	45.	3	15.	3	15.
T	2	18.1	3	27.3	0	0.	3	27.3	3	27.3
Total	56	12.2%	65	14.1%	142	31.3%	47	10.4%	144	32.0%

One hundred and forty-two colleges, or almost one-third of those responding, indicate that from 36 to 50 hours in the methods course are spent on the teaching of literature. This is the equivalent of 12 to 16 weeks in courses that meet 3 hours per week, far greater than the median of 3 to 5 weeks spent on composition or the median of 3 weeks spent on grammar.

---

[19] See page 71.
[20] See, for example, Kenneth Oliver, "Are English Teachers Properly Prepared?" *CTA Journal*, Vol. 55, No. 5 (May, 1959), pp. 22-23.

Summary

The survey reveals that, insofar as required offerings are considered, the preparation of secondary teachers in literature is more adequate than is the preparation in language. The most notable deficiencies are in the areas of world literature and contemporary literature and in the apparent indifference of colleges to educating teachers in methods of literary criticism. The overwhelming majority of colleges do not require a course in literature for adolescents. Although students may elect work of these kinds in most institutions, the absence of any widely held requirements suggests that existing programs in teacher education tend to neglect preparation in these areas.

Conclusion

The evidence presented here demonstrates the nationwide need for more highly qualified teachers of English. Between 40 and 60 per cent of the secondary teachers now teaching English do not possess a major in the subject. Many of those who do possess a major are inadequately prepared for the task of teaching English. In some states elementary teachers can be certified with little or no work in English. Ways must also be found to improve the preparation of practicing teachers of English. In many localities salaries are so low that teachers must accept evening jobs and summer positions to provide for themselves and their families. One study reports the average salary of the American public school teacher to be from $4,250 to $4,375 for those with only the bachelor's degree, the group which most needs additional study.[21] Another finds the national average in 1960 to be $4,109 for beginning teachers with bachelor's degrees.[22] Many practicing teachers would engage in further study of English if they could afford the time and money.

Special provisions are needed, too, to help those persons who are now teaching English with less than a college major. School board rulings and university regulations often prevent such teachers from pursuing additional study in English. On the one hand, local boards frequently accept credit for only graduate courses in awarding salary increments; on the other, the universities refuse to admit to graduate standing persons who lack the necessary undergraduate prerequisites. Thus, non-

---

[21] "Scheduled Salaries Continue to Rise," *Research Bulletin*, Research Division of the National Education Association, Vol. 38, No. 3 (October, 1960), p. 75.

[22] Letter from George S. Reuter, Jr., Research Director, American Federation of Teachers, November 10, 1960, based on data in George S. Reuter, Jr., *Survey of Teachers Salaries*, September, 1960 (Chicago, Ill.: American Federation of Teachers, 1960), pp. 51-75.

majors who are teaching English are discouraged from improving their preparation in subject matter. A similar problem is faced by many elementary teachers who could profit by enrolling in upper division courses in English but who lack the necessary preparation for graduate study in language and literature. This deep seated malpractice can be remedied, and the teaching of English can be improved, only by a program national in its scope which constantly focuses the light of public attention upon the best practices in the nation—a program which enlists the cooperative efforts of teachers in all segments of the school system, local boards, and the best minds in state departments of education.

THE NEED FOR BETTER TEACHING CONDITIONS

In recent years the teaching of English in American schools has sometimes been labeled ineffective. Our high school graduates, it has been said, neither read well nor write well at a time when the comprehension of the printed page and the expression of ideas in written and spoken words are of greater significance than at any past period of history. Teachers of English find it difficult to refute these accusations because they know better than anyone else that the teaching of English has not been as effective as it should be, albeit that some high school graduates do read and write with real competence. These same teachers of English also know better than anyone else that vast numbers of them have been working under conditions so difficult as to preclude the possibility of genuine effectiveness of instruction, especially in having students express their thoughts understandably in writing without glaring errors in their language.

Writing cannot be well taught unless teachers can read student papers. Reading cannot be well taught unless books are available for students. Studies of present conditions indicate that many teachers of English have neither the time nor the books to teach as effectively as they would like. This section reviews what is known about the load of English teachers and the availability of libraries and textbooks. It then reviews one consequence of inadequate instruction—the cost in time and money of remedial instruction in English at the college level. Finally, by assessing conditions in schools that produce superior English students, it suggests some standards toward which high schools may work.

THE CONDITIONS UNDER WHICH ENGLISH IS TAUGHT

Highlights

Research demonstrates that greater learning occurs in small classes.

Teachers who meet about 150 students daily require more than 50 hours a week just to meet classes and mark compositions. This allows no time for other important responsibilities.

Specialists in English consider four classes of 25 students each as the teaching load necessary for effective learning.

The present overload of teachers of English prevents students from receiving needed instruction and discourages recruitment.

Chief among unfavorable conditions is the load of the teacher of English. Teacher-load is a combination term referring to the entire effect of such factors as the total number of students a teacher has in his classes each day, the number of students he has in each class under his instruction, the number of class hours he teaches, the number of different grade levels—the number of preparations—for which he prepares daily, the number of out-of-class activities he sponsors, and others. The load of the teacher of English has been so heavy for so long that it has militated against attracting the best young people, or a sufficient quantity of them, into the profession. It has become an educational tradition to accept the fact that the English teacher must work under impossible conditions. It has even become normal practice that he will have in his classes—at least five in number—at least thirty students per class, for a grand total of at least 150 students per day, and it has not been unusual to find that total much greater. In addition, the English teacher has regularly coached plays and trained debating teams and students preparing for all sorts of programs—reading contests, public speaking contests, commencement programs, and similar activities—while he has also sponsored school newspapers, magazines, and annuals, not to mention certain other kinds of activities entirely unrelated to his basic work of teaching English.

Teaching load is heavy

Why Smaller Classes?

But why does it make any difference how many students an English teacher has? So long as there are enough seats in the classroom, why cannot a teacher handle thirty students per class as easily and as well as twenty-five? Thirty-five as easily and as well as thirty? Forty as easily and as well as thirty-five? Why cannot he handle two hundred students per day as easily and as well as one hundred?

There are two very definite answers to these questions. The first concerns class size as it relates to all teaching, and the second concerns class size and total number of students as they relate to the specific responsibility of the English teacher. The Metropolitan School Study Council, through the Institute of Administrative Research of Teachers College, Columbia University, has summarized and analyzed critically a body of research dealing with the question of class size and its relationship to teaching.[1] Many studies of class size have been made. Of the older ones

Class size affects learning

---

[1] D. H. Ross and Bernard McKenna, *Class Size: The Multi-Million Dollar Question*, Institute of Administrative Research, Teachers College, Columbia University, Study No. 11, 1955.

many were faulty in their research techniques. Those judged to be valid by the study group favored small classes by a *five* to *one* ratio.[2]

Newer studies have been more analytical of classroom practices in small and large groups and have reached conclusions like these:

> 1. Given a generally competent staff, the smaller the classes the greater the chance for invention and early adoption of newer and better practices.
> 2. Desirable classroom practices tend to be dropped when class size is increased; desirable practices are added when class size is reduced.
> 3. Small high school classes that are small by design and not by accident tend to have more variety in instructional methods than do large classes.
> 4. Small classes prevent "educational accidents." More attention to individuals is likely to be found in smaller groups.[3]

This report of the Metropolitan School Study Council gives a description in detail of the kinds of effective procedure that appear in small classes and not in large ones. During the past decade emphasis was laid upon teaching students according to their differing abilities. This emphasis is likely to continue. The cry for educating gifted children in keeping with their giftedness must be heeded, but so must the demand that *each* child be taught well. Even though children may be grouped into classes in accord with their abilities (homogeneous or ability grouping), these children must still be taught as individual persons. At every turn smaller classes are indicated as a way to prevent fitting every student into the same mold. Class size does, then, have a distinct relationship to good and effective teaching.

Written Composition—The English Teacher's Special Task

The whole matter of class size is closely related to the total number of students with whom an English teacher must deal. But it is this total itself that comes into prominence when we consider one of the major tasks of the English teacher: that of teaching his students to put words onto paper in such a way that they express ideas well and thus communicate these ideas to others. Teaching writing, as this effort is frequently called, involves what has always seemed an endless amount of time, so endless, indeed, that the English teacher has had to govern the time he devotes to this task not by the amount needed to do an effective job but by the amount of time at his disposal, in keeping with all the other tasks he must perform—in short, in view of the amount of his teaching load.

Writing requires correction

The English teacher is unique among teachers in that he alone bears the major responsibility of directing writing improvement. Of course, all

---
[2] *Ibid.*, p. 2.
[3] *Ibid.*, pp. 7-11.

teachers should promote the use of good English in all writing, but it is the English teacher who must perform the slow, arduous task of laboring with individual students over a long period of time as they gradually improve in expressing thmselves in written language.

How Much Writing?

Frequent writing is necessary

Under the sponsorship of the California Councils of Teachers of English, William J. Dusel has supplied exact information as to the time it takes to work with student writing. Everyone agrees that a person learns to write by writing. Everyone agrees, too, that someone must read that writing, react to it, and make suggestions for improvement. Nearly everyone agrees, too, that while it might be better to have students write more often, it is essential that they have a theme-type assignment once a week. The Harvard report, *General Education in a Free Society*, recommends "constant writing" as essential to improve writing at the secondary school level.[4] One experiment investigated the effect of the amount of writing on quality of writing and discovered that doubling the quantity reduced failures 66 per cent and improved grades 60 per cent.[5] Four hundred thirty experienced teachers and educators of national prominence agreed in Dusel's California study that high school students should write at least once a week—150 words for freshmen and 350 words per week for seniors.[6] The over-all average amount recommended by most teachers was 250 words each week for each pupil.

Marking Papers

But what does a teacher need to do with this quantity of writing? How does it affect his time? Everyone agrees that some competent person must supervise and guide students' writing if they are to improve in written expression. It is generally felt that an essential part of this process is to mark papers, that is, to read the papers over and note comments upon them. Ideally, the best supervision would be through regular and frequent individual conferences with all students, but this procedure is impossible, and marking papers must do. On this point Dusel wrote:

> But because the typical secondary school English teacher has five or six daily classes of thirty or more pupils each to instruct, he cannot offer very much

---

[4] Harvard University Committee on General Education, *General Education in a Free Society* (Cambridge, Mass.: Harvard University Press, 1946), pp. 11, 12.

[5] Virginia Lokke and George Wykoff, "Doubling Writing in Freshman Composition Experiment," *School and Society*, LXVIII (Dec. 18, 1948), pp. 437-439.

[6] William J. Dusel, "Determining an Efficient Teaching Load in English," *Illinois English Bulletin*, March, 1956, p. 4.

of this kind of service. Instead he must read his daily accumulation of papers after school hours, when pupils are not about; and he must depend on brief written comments to communicate his reactions and suggestions.[7]

How Long Does Marking Papers Take?

How much time does marking 250 papers weekly take? As with services of all kinds, how long a job takes depends directly on how well the job is done. Dusel had the 430 participating teachers submit samples of the procedures they used in marking a paper and an exact report of the time taken in this kind of marking. Some teachers did such a poor job of marking that it might even have been better not to return the papers to the students. Essentially all these teachers did was to assign a grade; there was little if anything to indicate to the student how to improve his writing. Yet even this kind of marking took 3.5 minutes per paper, or 8.8 hours per week, based on 150 papers from 150 students.[8]

Paper correction takes time

But no one wishes to foster this kind of useless and inefficient procedure on the part of any English teacher. Dusel found that effective marking of papers, designated as "marking to teach writing and thinking," took 8.6 minutes for a 250-word paper, or 21.5 hours per week for 150 papers.[9]

A glance at Dusel's report as summarized in the *Illinois English Bulletin* for March 15, 1956, or a look at recommendations for marking compositions in "Principles and Standards in Composition for Kentucky High Schools and Colleges," *Kentucky English Bulletin*, Fall, 1956-57, will show in detail the kind of marking an English teacher ought to do.[10]

The time total of 21.5 hours is still not all, though, for papers marked but thrown away by students do little good. Students must correct their papers, and the teacher must check the corrected work. This checking added 2.8 minutes per paper to the total time, 7 more hours per week.[11]

---

[7] *Ibid.*, p. 5.
[8] *Ibid.*, p. 7.
[9] *Ibid.*, p. 13.
[10] "Principles and Standards for Kentucky High Schools and Colleges." *Kentucky English Bulletin*, Vol. 6, No. 1, Fall, 1956-57 (Frankfort: State Department of Education, 1956).
[11] Dusel, *op. cit.*, p. 14.

The English Teacher's Work-Week

"Totaling the hours required for these duties," Dusel concluded, "indicates the magnitude, in work hours, of the job of teaching writing effectively, under present conditions of instruction, in California secondary schools."[12] Here is the total:

        25.0 hours per week of assigned English classes (the mode class load)

        21.5 hours of marking compositions (to teach writing and thinking)

        7.0 hours of checking the corrections or revisions of these compositions

        53.5 hours per week

less 2.7 hours available for correcting during class hours

tot. 50.8 hours of academic work per week required to meet classes and mark compositions effectively

plus ? hours for lesson planning and preparation for teaching the other skills and knowledge expected of the English program.

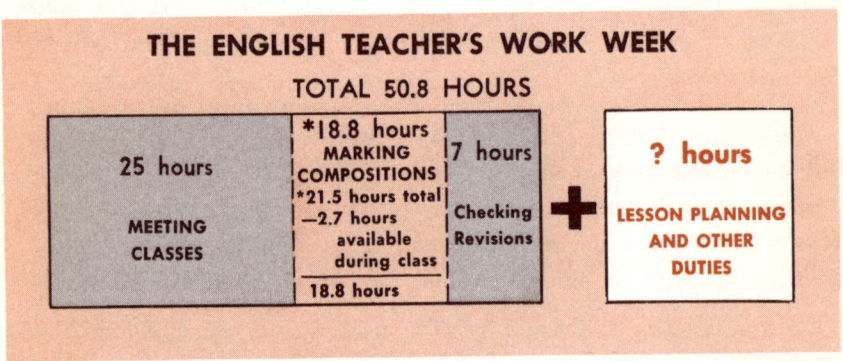

A similar summary is available for another state across the continent from California. From figures given in a Virginia study the following estimates represented the weekly effort of the hypothetical typical Virginia English teacher:[13]

---

[12] *Ibid.*, p. 15.
[13] E. M. Bowers and R. L. Norris, *Study of Teacher Load of Teachers of English in Virginia, 1958-59*, Bulletin, Virginia Association of Teachers of English, pp. 22-26.

1. Classroom teaching .... 25 hours
2. Holding study hall .... 5 hours
3. Preparing lessons .... 5 hours
4. Reading examinations, exercises, and themes .... 8 hours
5. Performing clerical duties .... 4 hours
6. Directing homeroom activities .... ½ hour
7. Performing other duties .... 1½ hours
    Total .... 49 hours

If we replace four of the hours indicated above for reading examinations, exercises, and themes by the 24.2 hours indicated by Dusel, then the total work-load of the Virginia teacher becomes 45 hours plus 24.2 hours, or 69.2 hours per week. In other words, it would take about seventy hours per week to do the job as it should be done.

Even then it appears that three major activities that are expected of the English teacher have not been included: (1) miscellaneous school system obligations expected of teachers in all subjects, like attending PTA meetings or contributing to general curriculum planning on both a school and system-wide basis; (2) coaching and directing students' activities like plays and speech contests, responsibilities for which the English teacher can be uniquely, and sometimes solely, qualified; and (3) what is generally thought of as "keeping up" in one's field, like reading new books by authors at both the adult and the student level of interest, becoming acquainted with basic research in the teaching of English, and participating in various professional activities.

In regard to another phase of the English teacher's task, Kansas and Indiana teachers were asked how many students they could teach in a class and still provide adequate speaking practice for all. Kansas teachers said that 17 students per class on an average would be necessary to accomplish this objective;[14] Indiana answers averaged 18.[15] In addition, Kansas teachers stated that in order to assign one theme per week they should average not more than 21 students per class.[16] Indiana teachers felt that under existing conditions they had time to "grade" only 57 themes per week as an average.[17] Thirty-three per cent of the teachers indicated less than 50 themes; 23 per cent said between 50 and 100.

Clearly, teaching loads must be held within reason if the desired learning is to take place.

---

[14]Ingrid M. Strom, *Teaching Load of Teachers of English in Indiana*, Bulletin of the School of Education, Indiana University, Vol. 32, No. 3 (May, 1956), p. 33.
[15]*Ibid.*, pp. 48, 49.
[16]Ibid., p. 22.
[17]*Ibid.*, p. 48.

Teacher-Load Studies and Statements

For many years English teachers have of necessity, though reluctantly, accepted their lot. Now, though, English teachers themselves are bringing these conditions to the attention of professional and lay people. The National Council of Teachers of English passed resolutions in 1956, 1957, and 1958 recommending that the over-all assigned load of the high school English teacher be limited to four classes of not more than 25 students in each class and that out-of-class responsibilities be substantially reduced so that each teacher might better devote himself to the thoughtful teaching of language and literature. Studies have been made in several states, cities, and counties to call attention to actual numbers of students and other load conditions faced by English teachers in these particular areas. Notable among the states are California, Georgia, Illinois, Indiana, Kansas, Michigan, Pennsylvania, and Virginia, states having a wide geographical spread. State English associations have passed resolutions similar to that of the National Council of Teachers of English. The Virginia Association, for example, as a part of a teacher-load study released in the fall of 1959, stated the following recommendation to school administrators:

Recommend four classes of 25 students each

> As a guide to making teaching assignments, administrators should consider the following schedule patterns appropriate for the usual six-period day in Virginia high schools:
> a. 4 English classes of 25 students each, 1 period free for conferences and planning, and 1 period for study hall supervision.
> b. 5 English classes of 20 students each and 1 period free for conferences and planning.[18]

On October 22, 1960, the New England Association of Teachers of English unanimously supported the following resolution:

> Resolved, that the NEATE endorse the proposition that the successful teaching of English may be expected only when the teacher of English has a class load of not more than four classes of twenty-five each and non-English assignments not to exceed homeroom and the equivalent of one hour of non-teaching duty during the school day.

Teachers at the local level identify this same problem. When Gary, Indiana, English teachers gave their reactions in a recent study, one of them wrote: "A rather worn-out criticism is that English teachers fail to provide students with the opportunity to express themselves in writing. Like most English teachers, I stand indicted on this count, not because of indifference to theme writing, but because of physical impossibilities

---

[18] Bowers and Norris, *op. cit.*, p. 1.

of a 24-hour day." Another Gary teacher said, simply, "We fail to do enough written work because of lack of time for correcting papers."[19]

Teachers of Jackson County, Kansas, in their recent report on teacher load used these words:

> What can be done to enable the English teacher to do his proper job, a job that so urgently needs doing? This committee believes that the action required, the measure of overriding importance, is the reduction of the teaching load of the English teacher to a maximum of 100 students.[20]

In October, 1959, the Cincinnati Committee on Teacher Load of the Superintendent's Advisory Council of Professional Staff Members reported findings of a study on teacher load. Teachers ranked ten "deterrents to good teaching" in the order of their bad effect.[21] Overcrowded classrooms ranked second only to the problem of dealing with all kinds of problem children (maladjusted, uninterested, hungry, physically handicapped, irresponsible, uncooperative).

Teachers of English are not alone in their sensitivity to the serious nature of the prevailing situation. The National Commission of Teacher Education and Professional Standards made the following recommendation in 1947:

> Twenty-five pupils should be the maximum number enrolled in any class or grade taught by one teacher; the total number of pupil-class enrollments taught by a teacher of academic subjects in secondary or departmentalized schools should not exceed one hundred per day.[22]

A committee of college personnel dealing with the education of California teachers recommended in 1947 that "the teacher of English should be assigned no more than four classes daily, with a total maximum enrollment of one hundred pupils daily."[23] Also, in 1954 the American Association of School Administrators joined with the Research Division of the National Education Association in stating that " a modern school program with its variable and complex objectives cannot be fully achieved when classes enroll more than 25 pupils."[24] In 1959, James B. Conant's *The American High School Today* was presented to the American people as a report on conditions with recommendations for improve-

---

[19] Unpublished (duplicated) report of the Gary, Indiana, English Council.
[20] *Report of the Jackson County Teachers of English Committee on Teacher Load* (mimeographed), p. 6.
[21] *Report of the Committee on Teacher Load to the Superintendent's Advisory Council of Professional Staff Members*, English Club of Greater Cincinnati (mimeographed), p. 16.
[22] Willard E. Givens, *Our Teachers: Annual Report of the Profession to the Public* (Washington, D. C.: National Education Association, 1947), p. 13.
[23] Alfred Grommon, "The Training of Teachers of English for the Secondary Schools of California," *The Educational Forum*, XII, November, 1947, p. 102.
[24] "Size of Class in 110 Urban School Districts over 100,000 in Population," *Education of Research Service*, a Monthly Report prepared by the American Association of School Administrators and the Research Division of the National Education Association, Circular No. 6 (Washington, D. C.: American Association of School Administrators, June, 1954), p. 9.

ment and was based on actual observations in schools by the author. Conant recommended that, in order to make correction and discussion of themes possible, teachers of English should be responsible for no more than 100 students.[25]

The Aim—To Improve Instruction

Like Dr. Conant, teachers of English are seeking to bring about effective instruction. They stand ready, eager to do their part. Typical thinking is reflected in a resolution of the Michigan Council of Teachers of English, as follows: "That as administrative action is taken to reduce over-all loads, teachers assume the responsibility for adopting classroom procedures that will permit thoughtful individualization of instruction, including weekly compositions carefully commented on by the teacher and subsequently corrected by the student."[26] The teacher-load study made in Michigan in 1959 ended with the vigorous conclusion that "the teaching loads of English teachers must be drastically reduced if the effectiveness of their teaching is to be increased or even preserved. They should teach fewer classes. They should teach fewer students. And they should be asked to be responsible for fewer activities."[27]

Reasonable loads will improve instruction

Facts about the English Teacher's Load

In view of these published pronouncements of national and state groups of teachers of English, it is only fair to ask why they are so concerned. The states and school districts listed in these tabulations have supplied the answer in much significant factual information, all gathered within recent years.

Number of classes taught— Most teachers of English teach five classes per day, for the five school days per week, in addition to other duties, chief among which is holding at least one study hall daily. For example, most Georgia teachers reported spending 25 hours weekly in the English classroom.[28] Of two hundred and eleven Pennsylvania English teachers reporting in 1958, 34 per cent taught at least six classes per day.[29] As many as 25 per cent of the teachers in Indiana also taught at least six classes daily.[30] In all states there were many with more than five classes daily.

[25]James B. Conant, *The American High School Today* (New York: McGraw-Hill Book Company, Inc., 1959), p. 31.
[26]Resolution Adopted by the Michigan Council of Teachers of English, 1959 (one-page leaflet).
[27]"Preparation and Pupil Load," *Newsletter of the Michigan Council of Teachers of English*, Vol. VI, No. 4, p. 12.
[28]Paul Farmer and Bernice Freeman, *The Teaching of English in Georgia*, A Report of the Georgia English Commission (Atlanta, Ga.: The Georgia Council of Teachers of English, 1952), pp. 13-20.
[29]Progress Report of the Committee on Teacher Load of the Pennsylvania Council of Teachers English, unpublished leaflet, 1958.
[30]Strom, *op. cit.*, p. 33.

Number of students per teacher per day—

In general most teachers have well over one hundred students per day. In Virginia the majority had 121 to 160 students per day.[31] In Indiana 28 per cent had between 150 and 199, and 2 per cent had over 200.[32] In Pennsylvania, the average was 166 pupils per day.[33] In Michigan, schools graduating over 300 students had 71.3 per cent of their English teachers with over 95 students per day; schools slightly smaller had 82.9 per cent with over 95. The over-all average teacher-pupil load was 126.[34]

Size of classes—

In California the median size of high school English classes was 30.8, meaning that about 50 per cent of classes were larger than this figure; but one-fourth of the classes had more than 35 students.[35] In Michigan the average English class size was 28.29;[36] in Gary, Indiana, 30.[37] To produce these averages, numerous classes must have had more than 30 students.

Lesson preparations—

Most English teachers report at least three daily lesson preparations. In Virginia, teachers have classes on at least three grade levels.[38] In Michigan the majority of those who teach English also have at least one class in some other subject.[39] Even when a teacher has two classes at the same grade level, it must be remembered, the teacher does not necessarily make the same preparation for both classes; more often the classes do not have the same assignments at the same time.

Other duties—

State association studies report time spent in various additional duties and activities such as reading examination papers, checking exercise material, reading themes, homeroom activities, clerical duties, attending a number of different kinds of meetings, even chaperoning, and looking after various "drives."

---

[31] Bowers and Norris, *op. cit.*, p. 18.
[32] Strom, *op. cit.*, p. 35.
[33] Progress Report of the Committee on Teacher Load of the Pennsylvania Council of Teachers of English, unpublished leaflet, 1958.
[34] "Preparation and Pupil Load," *Newsletter of the Michigan Council of Teachers of English*, Vol. VI, No. 4, p. 15.
[35] "California Teachers: Their Professional Qualifications, Experience, and the Size of their Classes, 1956-57," *Bulletin of the California State Department of Education*, Vol. XXVII, No. 10 (October, 1958), Sacramento, California, p. 50.
[36] "Preparation and Pupil Load," *Newsletter of the Michigan Council of Teachers of English*, Vol. VI, No. 4, p. 10.
[37] Unpublished (duplicated) report of the Gary, Indiana, English Council.
[38] Bowers and Norris, *op. cit.*, p. 20.
[39] "Preparation and Pupil Load," *Newsletter of the Michigan Council of Teachers of English*, Vol. VI, No. 4, p. 15.

How Many Students?

Obviously a reduction in the teaching load will not in itself ensure better English teaching. Teachers will still have a responsibility to see that their time is used wisely and well. Yet, the various facts brought out in studies referred to here show clearly that the situation in English teaching is serious and requires immediate attention. Most of these studies agree that an absolute maximum of 100 students per day taught in not over five classes, but preferably in four, should constitute the student load of the high school English teacher. The final paragraph of the report on Dusel's California study provides a fitting conclusion for this section of this monograph:

Reduce loads so students will learn

> The inevitable question arises: "How can we afford more English teachers?" The answer can only be that literacy is a first essential, not a luxury, in a democracy. People responsible for teaching such important and complex skills as reading and writing should be assigned only the number of pupils that they can teach effectively. The essential work of marking weekly compositions severely limits this number.[40]

THE INADEQUACY OF SCHOOL LIBRARY AND BOOK RESOURCES

> **Highlights**
>
> 10,000,000 elementary and about 150,000 high school students attend schools which lack central libraries.
>
> The average annual amount per pupil spent on library books is about half the estimated cost of one book.
>
> States spend an annual average of only $2.71 per pupil on free textbooks.

Despite spectacular advances in educational television, audio-visual aids, and other electronic teaching devices, reading remains the student's major avenue to learning. Whether in English, chemistry, history, or mathematics, the book remains the instrument through which the ideas and information of one generation are transmitted to the next. To limit a student's access to books is to limit his access to the best that is known and thought in the world. Yet in some communities a perilous disregard of school and classroom libraries undermines the educational program.

Millions of children lack libraries

---

[40] Dusel, *op. cit.*, p. 19.

Ten million elementary children are attending schools which do not have centralized school libraries.[41] Almost 150,000 secondary school students attend high schools which lack central libraries. Almost 500,000 in addition attend combined elementary-secondary schools which do not have central libraries. These are official figures reported in October, 1960, by the United States Office of Education after a careful survey of conditions in 15,526 school districts. Although the secondary schools without libraries total only 3.33 per cent of those surveyed, the fact that as many as 150,000 boys and girls are attending such schools is a matter for serious concern. Sixty-five per cent of the elementary schools and 12.3 per cent of the combined groups are without centralized libraries.

The findings of educational research and the experiences of successful teachers have long revealed that extensive reading by students is crucial in developing vocabulary, in introducing each child to increasingly mature ideas, and in serving as the foundation for later writing and thinking. Teachers in all academic subjects, and in many nonacademic, recognize the supreme importance of independent reading and library research in mastering the content of a subject.

Acting in cooperation with nineteen other professional societies, including the National Council of Teachers of English, the American Association of School Librarians published during 1960 an important report on minimum standards for school libraries.[42] The following table presents a comparison of the recommended minimum standards with the actual conditions found in American schools in 1958-1959.

---

[41]These and other statistics on current library resources are taken from Mary Helen Mahar and Doris C. Holladay, "Public-School Library Statistics, 1958-59," *Library Statistics*, U. S. Department of Health, Education, and Welfare, October, 1960.

[42]American Association of School Librarians, *Standards for School Library Programs* (Chicago: American Library Association, 1960). All standards mentioned in this report are taken from this book.

A COMPARISON OF RECOMMENDED STANDARDS AND ACTUAL PRACTICE IN PUBLIC SCHOOL LIBRARIES, 1958-1959

Standard	Recommended Minimum	National Average	Actual Practice Average, Elementary Schools	Average, High Schools	Average, Combined
Number of books per pupil	10 books per pupil	5.3	4.6	6	5.6
Annual expenditure per pupil for library books	minimum of $4.00-$6.00 per pupil	$1.60	$1.60	$1.85	$1.45
Personnel	100% of schools with libraries (One librarian for first 900 pupils; one for each 600 pupils thereafter)	42.4% of schools with librarians	25.8%	91.7%	76.7%

The above table presents an arresting comparison.

— The *minimum* recommended standard is *ten* library books per pupil.
— The *actual* average in American schools is 5.3 books per pupil.
— The *minimum* recommended standard is an annual expenditure of *$4.00-$6.00* per pupil on books.
— The *actual* national average is an annual expenditure of *$1.60* per pupil on books.

A telling commentary from the AASL report offers sufficient interpretation of these findings:

> It should be noted that the expenditure of the base minimum of $4.00 per student means that approximately one book per student can be added to the library each year. The current cost of books (allowing for discards) averaged $3.00 for the elementary school library, $3.50 for the junior high school library, and $4.00 for the senior high school library. Production costs of books have been rising steadily during the last decade, and there is every indication that costs will continue to mount.[43]

In many localities the supply of textbooks is inadequate as well. According to the 1955-56 Biennial Survey of Education in the United States, the state departments and intermediate boards of education, such as counties, in 42 states, reported expending $75,626,000 annually for free textbooks. This represents an average of $2.71 per pupil for all free textbooks supplied during a single year.[44] Although some local boards of

---

[43] *Ibid.*, p. 83.
[44] Based on data in Table 30, "Current Expenditures for Instruction in Full-time Public Elementary and Secondary Schools, by State: 1955-1956," *Statistics of State School Systems: Organization, Staff, Pupils, and Finances,* U. S. Office of Education, Chapter 2, pp. 88-89.

education undoubtedly supplement these expenditures, the fact remains that the average figure reported is less than the estimated cost of a single book.

One characteristic of a secondary school program that produces excellence in English is a plentiful supply of good books, as is indicated clearly in a report later in this chapter.⁴⁵ Reliance on a single set of elementary readers or a single set of high school literary anthologies is far from sufficient in teaching English. A primary responsibility of the teacher of English is to bring young people into contact with books. This is possible only when an adequate reserve of books is available in the classrooms and in central libraries. Unless students have available an adequate supply of books for supplementary out-of-school reading, class instruction in reading will not produce results. Drill alone is not enough; students must be able to practice reading skills outside. Moreover, the quality of the books, especially the textbooks, needs to be carefully considered. Too many teachers are forced to rely on inaccurate, outdated, or inappropriate textbooks in language and literature.

Forums at the 1960 Golden Anniversary White House Conference on Youth recommended "That quality library facilities and services be provided in elementary and secondary schools and colleges and universities, to enable them to achieve standards of academic excellence."⁴⁶ At the present time our schools have a long way to go.

THE COST OF REMEDIAL ENGLISH AT THE COLLEGE LEVEL

> **Highlights**
>
> Eighty-seven per cent of American colleges test the competence of entering freshmen in using English. During 1960 the cost of this program probably exceeded $800,000.00.
>
> An estimated 150,000 students failed college English tests during 1960.
>
> Almost two-thirds of American colleges offer remedial work in English, although most colleges do not grant college credit for completing such work.
>
> The estimated annual cost of instruction in remedial English in American colleges today is $10,114,736.62.

To ascertain the scope and cost of remedial English at the college freshman level, a special questionnaire was sent to 1665 directors of freshman composition on October 1, 1960. Within forty-five days, 619 questionnaires had been returned, 37.2 per cent of the total.

---
⁴⁵See page 121.
⁴⁶Recommendation 225, *Composite Report of Forum Findings,* Golden Anniversary White House Conference on Children and Youth (Washington, D. C.: Government Printing Office, 1960), p. 28.

The directors of freshman composition specified the type of institution for which they were reporting as follows:

University (U)	104
Liberal Arts College (L)	267
Teachers College (TC)	70
Technical School (TS)	29
Junior College (JC)	149
Total (tot)	619

Whenever possible, the letter symbols shown above will be used in this report. The number of teachers colleges in the sampling seems somewhat higher than in the studies on the preparation of teachers reported earlier, probably because the classification was made by representatives of each school. Many respondents indicate that a school is a "teachers college" even when its name does not so indicate.

DOES THE INSTITUTION TEST THE COMPETENCE OF ENTERING FRESHMEN IN USING THE ENGLISH LANGUAGE?

	Yes	%[47]	No	%
U	90	86.5	14	13.5
L	231	86.5	36	13.5
TC	64	91.4	6	8.6
TS	20	69.0	9	31.0
JC	134	90.0	15	10.0
tot	539	87.1	80	12.9

The overwhelming majority of colleges of all types test entering freshmen on their use of the English language. The fact that so many institutions have this requirement testifies to the great emphasis that American colleges place on the ability of each student to use English.

HOW MANY STUDENTS WHO PLANNED TO ENTER COLLEGE IN THE FALL OF 1960 WERE TESTED?

	Less than 300 students	300-1000 students	over 1000 students
U	2	30	57
L	119	94	9
TC	17	32	12
TS	5	12	5
JC	71	44	17
tot	214	212	100

---

[47] All percentages in this chapter refer to the percentage of the total number of institutions responding (n = 619).

MEDIAN NUMBER OF STUDENTS TESTED

	Median	Range
U	1200	22 to 30,000
L	325	6 to 3,200
TC	510	30 to 1,500
TS	750	1 to 4,500
JC	279	14 to 5,400

Clearly, the testing of students' ability to use English is a major endeavor on the part of American colleges and universities. If the same number of students are tested at all institutions of higher education, more than 600,000 students were tested during 1960 alone.[48]

HOW MANY OF THESE STUDENTS FAIL THE EXAMINATION?

	Less than 50	50-100	101-300	Over 300
U	9	7	18	15
L	70	47	19	5
TC	12	8	10	5
TS	4	1	3	2
JC	34	24	10	17
tot	129	87	60	44

MEDIAN NUMBER OF FAILURES REPORTED

	Median	Range
U	200	25 to 12,000*
L	62	0 to 1,500
TC	120	15 to 484
TS	140	1 to 2,700
JC	95	0 to 1,656

(*The high figure reflects a statewide testing program.)

The variation in the median number of failures reported by different kinds of institutions probably reflects to some degree differing admission requirements as well as the differing sizes of the college student bodies. If the median number of failures reported by institutions in this survey

---

[48]Data on the total number of institutions of each type were taken from *Statistics of Higher Education: 1955-56, Biennial Survey of Education in the United States*, Chapter 4, Section 1 (Washington, D. C.: U. S. Department of Health, Education and Welfare, 1958).

holds true for all institutions of higher education, the total number of students who failed college English examinations during 1960 probably exceeded 150,000.

PERCENTAGE OF STUDENTS FAILING		
	Mean Percentage	Range
U	25.3	0% to 50%
L	23.3	0% to 65%
TC	24.2	10% to 66.6%
TS	44.2	1.5% to 100%
JC	19.6	0% to 66.6%

In most institutions somewhat more than 20 per cent of the tested students failed the examination in English during 1960. The percentage may be somewhat higher for technical colleges. However, a number of schools reported that as many as 50 per cent of those tested actually failed the examination.

What is the total annual cost of the testing program?

Institutions were asked to estimate the annual program for testing competence in English. Respondents were asked to include in their estimate the cost of procuring tests, of proctoring examinations, of grading and marking papers, of notifying students, and of providing for general administration of the program. Not all of the respondents were able to estimate costs. For those that did, the range of estimated costs was as follows:

Cost of testing varies with schools

ESTIMATED COST OF ENGLISH TESTING PROGRAM				
	Less than $100	$100 to $500	$501 to $1000	Over $1000
U	8	20	7	17
L	46	81	18	12
TC	11	22	7	3
TS	2	10	0	2
JC	30	29	7	9
tot	97	162	39	43

The cost varies considerably from school to school with the annual cost of testing in most colleges falling in the $100 to $500 range. However, in the larger schools, the cost often exceeds this amount as is indicated by the following data on mean expenditures at institutions of varying kinds.

MEAN ESTIMATED EXPENDITURE FOR TESTING DURING 1960

		Range
U	$1,669.10	$ 0 to $12,000.
L	603.86	0 to 30,000.
TC	428.93	30 to 1,500.
TS	6,360.66	50 to 50,000.*
JC	392.52	0 to 5,000.

(*Figures are skewed by estimates of $24,000 and $50,000 from two institutions unable to separate the cost of testing students in English from the cost of testing other aptitudes.)

The amounts that the institutions of higher learning spend on testing students in English vary from school to school. However, when the mean expenditure for each type of institution is compared with the mean number of students tested (reported earlier), it is possible to estimate the mean cost per student.

ESTIMATED MEAN COST PER STUDENT OF 1960 TESTING PROGRAM*

U	$1.39
L	1.86
TC	.84
JC	1.41

(*No figure is included for technical schools because the great variation in cost makes a mean figure unreliable.)

The mean figures suggest that in most institutions the annual cost of testing is about $1.40 per student or more. Only in the teachers colleges do costs appear to be substantially less than this amount. Since an estimated 600,000 students were tested in English during 1960, the annual cost of the testing program for English apparently exceeded $800,000.00.

DOES YOUR SCHOOL PROVIDE SPECIAL REMEDIAL INSTRUCTION FOR STUDENTS WHO ARE DEFICIENT IN THEIR USE OF ENGLISH?

	Yes		No	
U	62	59.6%	42	40.4%
L	150	56.2	117	43.8
TC	36	51.4	34	48.6
TS	16	55.2	13	44.8
JC	112	75.1	37	24.9
tot	376	60.7%	243	39.3%

Almost three-fifths of the institutions provide remedial instruction in English for students unable to meet college standards. The percentage of institutions offering such instruction is especially pronounced among the junior colleges, least so among the liberal arts schools. However, in every category more than half of the institutions offer such work.

HOW MANY STUDENTS WERE ENROLLED FOR SUCH REMEDIAL INSTRUCTION DURING THE FALL, 1960, SEMESTER?

	0 to 50 students		51 to 100		over 101	
U	11	10.6%	15	14.4%	35	33.7%
L	75	28.1	38	14.2	22	8.2
TC	16	22.8	10	14.3	14	20.0
TS	6	20.7	4	13.8	3	10.3
JC	43	28.8	22	14.7	46	30.9
tot	151	24.4%	89	14.4%	120	19.4%

In slightly less than one-fifth of all institutions responding, more than 100 students were enrolled in remedial English during the fall semester of 1960, whereas in slightly more than one-fourth of the schools fewer than 50 students were so enrolled. For the 60.7 per cent of the institutions reporting such remedial courses, the mean number of students enrolled is as follows:

MEAN STUDENT ENROLLMENT IN REMEDIAL ENGLISH (Fall, 1960)

	Mean No. Students	Range
U	216.5	22 to 1000
L	74.21	1 to 1100
TC	93.6	17 to 570
TS	73.7	25 to 183
JC	228.6	8 to 2500

The proportionately larger mean enrollments in junior colleges and in universities may reflect admission policies which are less selective than those of liberal arts colleges and technical schools.

HOW MANY FULL TIME FACULTY MEMBERS WERE ASSIGNED TO TEACH REMEDIAL COURSES DURING FALL, 1960?

	0 to 2 faculty members	3 to 5	6 or more
U	34	13	9
L	123	11	6
TC	31	3	1
TS	12	0	1
JC	79	22	8
tot	279	49	25

The overwhelming majority of institutions report assigning from 0 to 2 full time faculty members to teaching remedial English. The mean number of faculty members assigned in each type of school is indicated below.

MEAN NUMBER OF FULL TIME FACULTY MEMBERS ASSIGNED TO TEACH REMEDIAL ENGLISH

U	3.68
L	1.48
TC	1.47
TS	1.29
JC	2.34

The higher mean number of faculty members assigned to teaching remedial English in universities and junior colleges is a reflection of the greater number of remedial classes at these institutions.

WHAT IS THE AVERAGE ANNUAL SALARY OF A FULL TIME STAFF MEMBER (OR THE EQUIVALENT OF A FULL TIME STAFF MEMBER) ASSIGNED TO TEACH REMEDIAL ENGLISH?

	$0 to $2,000	$2,001 to $4,000	$4,001 to $6,000	Over $6,000
U	6	10	32	2
L	9	21	63	11
TC	2	0	14	12
TS	1	1	7	2
JC	5	14	25	35
tot	23	46	141	62

Although the average annual salaries vary considerably, more schools report salaries ranging between $4,000 and $6,000 than any other amount. The mean salaries reported paid by schools in each category are as follows:

	Mean salaries	Range
U	$4,558.75	$1,200 to $ 7,000.
L	4,658.22	1,000 to 7,200.
TC	5,848.00	600 to 11,000.
TS	4,620.00	2,400 to 6,000.
JC	$5,603.77	$1,500 to $ 7,800.

Annual costs of remedial English total over $10,000,000.

The mean salary of the instructor of remedial English ranges from about $4,500 to almost $5,800 annually, depending upon the type of institution in which he is located. Salaries for teachers of remedial English tend to be higher in the teachers colleges and the junior colleges than in other institutions, probably because the teaching of remedial English often is assigned to regular faculty members in such schools. In universities much of the teaching is assigned to graduate assistants and young instructors who are paid at minimum salaries.

Only about one-half of the responding institutions reported salary figures. Still the sampling is sufficiently large so that the data may be used as the basis for estimating the total instructional cost of remedial English in American colleges today.

THE ESTIMATED COST OF REMEDIAL ENGLISH

	Total number of colleges[49]	% offering remedial work	Estimated number offering remedial English	Mean No. of instructors	Mean salary per instructor
U	139	59.6	83	3.68	4,558.75
L	728	56.2	408	1.48	4,658.22
TC	192	51.4	99	1.47	5,848.00
TS	44	55.2	24	1.29	4,620.00
JC	503	75.1	377	2.34	5,603.77

---

[49]*Statistics of Higher Education: 1955-59, Biennial Survey of Education,* U. S. Department of Health, Education, and Welfare, 1958, p. 2.

ESTIMATED TOTAL ANNUAL INSTRUCTIONAL EXPENDITURE FOR REMEDIAL ENGLISH	
Universities	$ 1,393,288.60
Liberal Arts Colleges	2,812,819.56
Teachers Colleges	822,059.44
Technical Schools	143,035.20
Junior Colleges	4,943,533.82
Total Estimate	$10,114,736.62

According to estimates based on the data reported in this survey, over ten million dollars is being spent during the 1960-61 school year on salaries of instructors for remedial English at the college level. This is in addition to the estimated $800,000.00 expended on the testing program. Any substantial improvement in the teaching of high school should improve the preparation in English of college-bound students, decrease the number of students needing remedial work, release college teachers from such instruction, and save time and money for the institutions of higher learning.

DO STUDENTS AT YOUR INSTITUTION RECEIVE COLLEGE CREDIT FOR COMPLETING THE COURSE IN REMEDIAL ENGLISH?				
	Yes	%	No	%
U	24	23.1%	40	38.5%
L	55	20.6	92	34.5
TC	17	24.3	23	32.7
TS	1	3.5	13	48.3
JC	67	45.0	46	30.9
	164	26.5%	214	34.5%

College credit often withheld

Most institutions offering remedial English do not grant students college credit for completing the course. Except in the junior colleges, where student bodies often include many individuals enrolled in nonacademic as well as academic work, the institutions have the policy that remedial English is not college level work. The colleges that did not respond to this question (approximately 39%) were primarily those that do not offer remedial English.

ARE STUDENTS WHO TAKE REMEDIAL ENGLISH REQUIRED TO COMPLETE A YEAR OF FRESHMAN ENGLISH IN ADDITION TO THE REMEDIAL COURSE?

	Yes	%	No	%
U	52	49.9%	13	12.5%
L	109	40.8	34	12.7
TC	29	41.4	8	11.4
TS	15	51.7	0	0.0
JC	79	53.0	34	22.8
tot	284	45.9%	89	14.4%

The overwhelming majority of institutions offering remedial English require students to complete a year of freshman English in addition to the remedial course.

IS COMPLETION OF THE REMEDIAL COURSE ACCEPTED IN FULFILLMENT OF THE REGULAR REQUIREMENT FOR A YEAR OF FRESHMAN ENGLISH?

	Yes	%	No	%
U	11	10.6%	54	51.9%
L	31	11.6	114	42.7
TC	8	11.4	30	42.8
TS	0	0.0	15	51.7
JC	34	22.2	76	51.0
tot	84	13.6%	289	46.6%

Only 13.6 per cent of all institutions and fewer than one-fourth of the institutions offering a remedial English course permit students to substitute the course for regular work in English. This finding, together with the previous one, underscores the tremendous waste of time and energy involved in teaching such courses. Although two-thirds of our colleges find it necessary to offer such remedial work, most require students to enroll in "regular" English after the remedial work is completed.

Summary

The data in this survey reveal that remedial work in English is offered at three of every five colleges in the United States. Although most colleges do not grant credit for such work, they necessarily expend as much as ten to eleven million dollars annually in testing and teaching students. Although the scope and cost of remedial English at the college level offers no certain yardstick with which to measure the adequacy of high school programs, any substantial improvement in the teaching of English in secondary English classrooms would inevitably reduce the burden on the colleges and release instructors and funds for other important uses.

HIGH SCHOOLS THAT PRODUCE SUPERIOR ENGLISH STUDENTS[50]

> **Highlights**
>
> High schools that produce superior English students tend to:
>
> Require four years of English in grades 9, 10, 11, 12.
>
> Have lower than average English teacher loads.
>
> Have English teachers with strong college undergraduate preparation in English, and a sizable proportion with graduate work in English.
>
> Require considerable amounts of writing from students, with much of the writing on nonpersonal subjects.
>
> Offer English courses that balance instruction in literature and composition about evenly.
>
> Stress functional teaching of grammar, with exercises intended more to teach application than to teach identification.
>
> Follow a systematically planned course of study, but with a degree of freedom to accommodate individual differences in teachers and students.
>
> Have adequate supervision of English teaching.
>
> Have special provisions for instruction of academically talented students.
>
> Have adequate library facilities, reference books, classroom libraries, and audio-visual and other instructional aids.

What are the characteristics of superior high school English departments? No research studies have been made which provide definitive answers to this question. A complete answer would reveal the contri-

---

[50]This study was conducted under the direction of J. N. Hook.

bution of the superior department to the learnings and skills of every student, regardless of his native ability.

For one feature of the superior department, however, a measure of sorts is available and is presented here. It may be assumed that a superior department produces some students who are superior. The characteristics of departments that do prepare students who demonstrably read and write unusually well are outlined in this study.

Background

In 1958-59 and again in each of the two following years, the National Council of Teachers of English attempted systematically to discover the nation's outstanding high school English students. In mailings that went to all senior high schools in the United States, English departments were invited to nominate their best students. The incentive was that the NCTE would recommend to colleges that financial help be provided for the winners and runners-up among these exceptionally able students.

Each year the first screening took place in the individual competing high schools. A school with below 500 enrollment, in grades 10, 11, and 12 combined, was entitled to one nominee; a school with 500 to 999 students, to two nominees; and so on up to schools with above 3,000 enrollment, which could nominate seven students. Each school was urged to choose its best English student or students; the choice was determined by department vote or sometimes by preliminary competition within the school.

The judging of the nominees was performed by state committees under the guidance of the NCTE. Each nominee was asked to submit three pieces of writing: an autobiography, an example of the best composition of which he was capable, and an impromptu composition written under supervision in one hour on a topic designated by the NCTE. In addition, each nominee was given two standardized tests: a test of his ability to read and interpret literature, and a college level test of grammar, usage, punctuation, and other skills of composition. Finally, supporting letters from the nominee's teachers and administrators were included in the packet that went to the state judging team.

Most of the judges were college teachers, including many heads of college or university English departments and many chairmen of college freshman composition. A few judges were high school English teachers who have gained considerable prominence for the excellence of their teaching and their knowledge of their subject.

In the first year of the competition, approximately 2,300 students were nominated. In the second and third years, the number each year exceeded 4,000. Of these, a number of winners were selected in each state in proportion to the state's population. The maximum number for each state was the number of that state's Representatives in Congress. Each state was also entitled to a like number of runners-up.

As a result of the careful screening, the competition unquestionably discovered many of the nation's most able English students. Colleges quickly became interested. The first year's winners and runners-up received approximately $852,000 in aid, and when figures can be compiled for later years, the amount will probably be found to increase. One college, in the second year of the competition, earmarked $100,000 for the students who chose to attend that school. Others gave and are giving high priority to these students.

Fewer than a fourth of the winners and runners-up plan to major in English in college. Of 477 first-year winners and runners-up whom the NCTE has been able to check upon, 117 were planning during their freshman year to work toward a major in English, 114 were undecided, 30 were expecting to major in mathematics, 25 in foreign languages, 19 in engineering, 15 in physics, 15 in political science, 13 in chemistry, 13 in elementary education, 12 in premedical, and smaller numbers in each of 36 other fields.

The questionnaire to winning schools

After the second year of the competition, the NCTE decided to send a questionnaire to the heads of the English departments in the schools from which winners and runners-up had come. The purpose was to discover, in as much detail as possible, the characteristics of the English departments of these schools. It was assumed that exceptionally able students come, as a rule, from good schools and good departments (as well as from intellectually stimulating homes). If it proved possible to discover the kinds of schools and departments from which the superior English students come, guidelines might be established which would help other schools and other English departments to improve their offerings.

Replies on 746 questionnaires were tabulated, representing over 90 per cent of the schools that had winners or runners-up in 1958-59 or 1959-60. The following analysis summarizes and comments upon the replies to the fifteen individual questions. Ambiguous answers and failures to answer have been ignored in the tabulation.

1. ENROLLMENT

Your school's enrollment as of September, 1959, in grades 10, 11, and 12 combined.

Size	Number responding
Below 500	236
500-999	159
1,000-1,499	165
1,500-1,999	99
2,000-2,499	38
2,500-2,999	34
3,000 or over	14

Comment: The size of a school, judging from these results, has no definite bearing upon its ability to produce superior English students. The fact that almost a third of the winners and runners-up come from schools of below 500 reveals that, given the right conditions, these schools may teach no less effectively than larger schools.

2. REQUIRED ENGLISH

A. Are all students in your school required to earn four full-year English credits in grades 9, 10, 11, 12?

Yes	No
500	185

Comment: It seems significant that four full-year English credits are required in over 73 per cent of the schools that produced these superior students.

B. Are journalism and speech courses counted as English credits?

Yes	No	Journalism but not speech	Speech but not journalism
179	447	16	25

Comment: The purpose of this question was to discover whether in these schools "English" means English in the limited sense or whether these two important but peripheral areas were counted as English. It is noteworthy that in 67 per cent of these schools, "English" is English in the conventional definition of the term, and speech or journalism courses are not included.

3. CLASS SIZE

What is the average size of English classes in your school?	
Size	Number of responses
Below 20	23
20-24	73
25-29	298
30-34	119
35-40	55
over 40	7

Comment: The median class size in these schools which produced demonstrably superior students is 25-29. Yet in school after school throughout the United States the class is 35, 40, or even more. The data presented earlier indicate that the median size in most states is around 30.[51] Thus half of the English classes enroll more than 30 students. Earlier in this section the demands for the paper grading and checking of revised papers in a well-taught English class were discussed. According to the research of Dusel, a teacher with 5 classes of 30 to 35 students each must spend 28.5 hours a week in marking and commenting upon papers.[52] This, added to 25 hours in class and 10 to 15 hours for other school-connected activities, means a work week of 63 to 68 hours. In contrast, the teacher who has 5 classes of 25 students must spend 1000 minutes (16-2/3 hours) in evaluation and has a somewhat more reasonable work week of 52 to 57 hours. For teachers with 4 classes, the work week is reduced to 45 to 50 hours. In actuality, even dedicated English teachers with large classes now assign fewer papers than they know they should, because they simply do not have enough time to evaluate papers every week; as a result, their students get too little practice in writing and do not learn to express themselves with accuracy, facility, and felicity. N.B. In Russian elementary and secondary schools in 1930, according to *Soviet Professional Manpower*, the ratio was 36 students per teacher; in 1940 it had declined to 28 to 1; in 1950, to 23 to 1.

Lower class size

---

[51]See page 99.
[52]See page 94.

4. NUMBER OF CLASSES PER TEACHER

Including both English and other subjects, what is the number of classes taught daily by a regular English teacher in your school?

Number of classes	Number of responses
3	9
4	79
5	529
6	65

Comment: As has already been reported, the NCTE by official resolution endorses a policy calling for an English teacher-load of 4 classes of no more than 25 students each. In most schools that produced superior students, the load is obviously heavier than that, but, combined with the average class size of 25 to 29, the total load is about 135 students per teacher, in comparison with the 175 or more in many of the nation's schools. In view of evidence that few schools yet assign only 4 classes to a teacher of English,[53] the finding of 79 such schools among the 682 responding is especially noteworthy.

5. OTHER ACTIVITIES

Approximately what is the average amount of time spent daily on extra-curricular activities, other school-connected activities, and lesson preparation by the typical English teacher in your school?

Amount of time	Number of responses
1 hour	95
2 hours	299
3 hours	185
4 hours	48
Over 4 hours	40

Comment: The drain of these activities on the teacher's time and energy is obvious. The median figure here is 2 hours a day or 10 hours a week; the average is somewhat higher. Yet for these schools that produced winners and runners-up, this figure appears to be lower than reported in other school surveys;[54] in some schools the English teacher's day is only well started when the closing bell rings, since he may still have remaining 5 or more hours of school-connected activities.

---

[53] See data on page 98.
[54] Virginia teachers reported about 3 hours daily spent holding study hall, performing clerical duties, directing homeroom activities, etc. See page 95.

6. AMOUNT OF STUDENT WRITING

In your school how much writing for teacher-criticism is done, in a typical week, by students in English classes in grades 10, 11, and 12? (This question refers to "themes" only, not sentence exercises, etc.)

Amount	Number of responses
Below 100 words a week	39
100-250 words	387
251-500 words	198
Over 500 words	39

Comment: The superior students learned to write because they had much practice in writing. Although the median of the responses is 100 to 250 words a week, it is significant that in 30 per cent of the schools answering this questionnaire the amount of writing averages 251 to 500 words and that in 6 per cent it averages over 500 words. This amount corresponds closely to the standard recommended earlier in this chapter.[55]

Frequent writing

7. PAPER-GRADING TIME

What is the average amount of time spent by each English teacher in your school in evaluating student writing?

Amount of time	Number of responses
0-3 hours a week	35
4-6 hours	202
7-9 hours	195
10-12 hours	147
Over 12 hours	83

Comment: The median here is 7 to 9 hours, but about 35 per cent of the teachers spend 10 hours or more. Less dedicated or more hard-pressed teachers probably spend much less time on this task, and as a result their students fail to learn to write well. (See once more the comment on Question 3.)

---

[55] See page 92.

8. LIBRARY FACILITIES

A. What is the estimated number of books in your school library?	
Number of books	Number of responses
Fewer than 4,000	147
4,000-6,000	171
6,000-10,000	191
10,000-20,000	142
20,000-30,000	10
More than 30,000	13

Comment: A well-stocked library is essential to a good English program. The median figure above is 6,000 to 10,000 books. Although the number of books needed varies with the size of the school, it is pertinent that the libraries in the schools from which these superior students come appear larger than the national average, even though 236 of the schools have enrollments below 500. (The American Library Association recommends 6,000 to 10,000 books for schools of 200 to 999 students; 10 books per student for schools over 1,000.)

Adequate libraries

B. How much reading room space is available for your students?	
Amount of space	Number of responses
For fewer than 25 students	54
For 25-50 students	194
For 50-100 students	270
For more than 100 students	168

Comment: A crowded library without adequate space for students to use books is of comparatively small value. The schools from which these superior students come provide reading room space for a median of 50 to 100 students, and about 25 per cent of them provide space for more than 100 students. Such facilities are conducive to browsing, reading, and elementary research. (The American Library Association recommends a minimum seating capacity of 45 to 55 in schools of 200 to 250, and 10 per cent of the enrollment in larger schools.)

C. In what kinds of classes does your school maintain classroom libraries? (Check one or more.)

Kind of classes	Number of responses
Few classes of any kind	320
Many English classes	249
Many science classes	148
Many social studies classes	175
Other	110

Comment: In addition to the general library, many good schools make worthwhile books even more accessible to students by providing classroom libraries. It appears significant that a high proportion of the schools from which superior English students come do offer these facilities.

9. SUBJECTS FOR STUDENT WRITING

Check the types of subjects on which students in grades 10, 11, and 12 write on frequently.

Type of subject	Number times checked
Literature	620
Science	197
Social studies	334
Art	65
Music	64
Personal interests	622
Other	169

Comment: These responses indicate the wide range of subject matter treated in student writing. The emphasis on "personal interest" topics is obviously high and is desirable for purposes of motivation. Nevertheless, the students in these schools write approximately as often on literary topics as they do on their possibly more personal concerns and frequently turn their attention to social studies, science, art, and music. Exclusive or almost exclusive attention to personal interest topics would be unfortunate because it would result in neglect of the objective, analytical kind of writing often required in college and in the reports and similar papers frequently needed in business and industry.

Balanced writing program

10. TEACHER BACKGROUND

Indicate the number of English teachers in your school of whom each statement is true.

Statement	Total number
_____have college undergraduate majors in English	4147
_____have college undergraduate minors in English	1112
_____have neither undergraduate majors nor minors in English	207
	5466
_____have no college degree	16
_____have a bachelor's degree (as the highest degree)	2563
_____have a master's degree in English	1553
_____have a master's degree in education	847
_____have a master's degree in another subject	357
_____have a doctor's degree	45
	5381

Well-prepared teachers

Comment: One of the generally recognized requirements for teaching a subject well is adequate knowledge of the subject. Much poor teaching of English is done by well-intentioned persons whose chief preparation is in other subjects; their students fail to learn much about English because their teachers do not know much about English (e.g., the teacher whose students learned that *July* "is an adverb because it ends in *-ly*"). The figures in the above table reveal that the English teachers in the schools from which superior students come are, on the whole, well prepared.

Of 5,466 of the teachers in the superior schools for whom information was made available, over 78 per cent majored in English during their college undergraduate years. This finding contrasts sharply with surveys showing that in most schools only 40 to 60 per cent of the English classes are taught by teachers with majors in English.[56] Fewer than 4 per cent of the teachers in superior schools earned neither an English major nor an English minor. Of the 5,381 concerning whom degree information was given, almost 29 per cent have a master's degree in English, and more than 15 per cent have a master's degree in education, which presumably included some specialized work in or related to English. The doctorate, rather rare in secondary schools, is surprisingly well represented in this group of schools.

---

[56]See data on pages 35-36.

11. LITERATURE AND COMPOSITION

A. In grades 10, 11, and 12, what is the approximate proportion of time devoted to literature?

Proportion of time	Number of responses
1/4	20
3/8	96
1/2	333
5/8	129
3/4	67
7/8	1

Comment: The majority of schools from which these superior students come devote approximately half their time to literature, half to composition broadly defined to include grammar, mechanics, speech activities, and the like. This does not imply, of course, that the year is divided into a semester of literature and a semester of composition, or that any similar arbitrary arrangement exists; often composition work grows naturally from the work in literature.

B. How is the work in literature in grades 10, 11, and 12 most often arranged? (Check one or two.)

Arranged	Number of responses
Chronologically	332
By literary types	378
However the text is arranged	87
By thematic units	180
Other	13

Comment: The responses and penciled comments show that the arrangement of the work in literature may shift from one year to the next. The thematic or the type arrangement is most prevalent in grade 10, the chronological in 11 (American literature) and 12 (English literature), although schools experiment with various combinations; for example, types are sometimes taught in a roughly chronological pattern.

C. In composition (broadly defined to include writing, grammar punctuation, spelling, etc.) to which of these does your school devote the most time?

Most emphasized in composition	Number of responses
1. Formal approach to grammar, with a systematic analysis of rules and principles and many identification exercises	61
2. Functional approach to grammar, with exercises intended more to teach application than to teach identification	216
3. Study of punctuation, spelling, and other mechanics	20
4. Study of structural or descriptive linguistics	5
5. Writing by students and discussion of what they write, along with discussion of professional authors' techniques	152
6. Workbook exercises	8
7. Other	3

Comment: A large number of responses were not tabulated here because more than a single answer was checked. Of the 465 that were tabulated, the numbers of responses to 2, 5, and 6 seem most significant. In many schools grammar is taught as mere *identification* of predicate nominatives and the like, but in the schools in this survey, almost four times as many stress *application* instead. Further, the emphasis on student writing and discussion in 152 schools may certainly suggest a reason for their having produced students who know how to write. Number 6 is noteworthy because only 8 schools among the 465 rely heavily upon workbook exercises.

12. COURSE OF STUDY

Does your school follow, in general, a course of study?	
Course of study	Number of responses
Prepared by high school department	293
Prepared by a city school system	96
Prepared by the state	67
None, but systematic departmental planning	65
None, but planning by individual teachers	73
Other	47

Comment: Only 73 of the schools reported that each teacher is a law to himself. The other 568 find it advantageous to have some over-all plan to follow, presumably to eliminate undesirable duplication or important omissions.

13. SUPERVISION

How is English teaching in your school district supervised? (Check one or more.)

| Method of supervision | Number of responses |

By department head	323
By principal or other administrative officer	314
By city language arts supervisor	71
By county or district supervisor	40
By state department of education	30
No supervision	96
Other	34

Comment: Although supervisory responsibilities follow no observable pattern, and in some schools are shared by two or more persons or groups, it is pertinent that some kind of supervision does exist in all but 96 of the schools reporting here. The laissez-faire doctrine, although it may result in some brilliant teaching, may also result in poor or uncoordinated teaching.

14. FACTORS INFLUENCING SUCCESS

To what factors do you attribute the success of your school in educating NCTE Achievement Awards winners?

Comment: The 669 free-response replies to this question reveal many of the characteristics of the schools which produced Award winners. Each usually named several factors. Many department heads modestly gave most of the credit to the individual students; in all, 257 responses praised the caliber of the student or students, a few saying that their students would have been Award winners regardless of their training in English classes. The following tabulation records other oft-repeated answers.

| | Number of free responses |

A. Well-prepared, dedicated teachers	289
B. Much emphasis on composition	250
C. Special attention to able students	197
D. Strong program in reading and literature	173
E. Emphasis on fundamentals of English	89
F. Superior homes and backgrounds of students	89
G. Carefully planned curriculum	69
H. Earlier preparation of students	52

I.	School emphasis on academic achievement	46
J.	Able administrators, interested in English	44
K.	Possession and use of a good library	39
L.	Community interest in education	33
M.	Reasonable teacher load	32
N.	School and departmental insistence on high standards	32
O.	Availability of educational materials	22
P.	Close cooperation of English teachers	20
Q.	Vocabulary work	20
R.	Others (fewer than 20 responses each)	193

Selected comments on the factors which cause success:

A. Well-prepared, dedicated teachers

"Teachers well educated in the field of English who have taught creatively to capture the students' interest and communicate a love for good literature." "Teachers with excellent backgrounds in reading and writing who encourage students to read, to write, and to think." "Our English teachers are teaching their major subject." "Dedication of individual English teachers to inspiring or requiring a high quality of performance from their respective students; a constant awareness that what they are doing must be constantly evaluated and re-evaluated as they encounter ideas new to them." "Skilled teachers who know good writing; teachers with the knack for writing." "There is no substitute for an adequately prepared staff."

B. Much emphasis on composition

"At least one theme per week." "An increasing emphasis on composition instruction has improved our program." "We stress not only writing but also revising composition. Students are made to feel that they need to say something and that they should say it as coherently and carefully as possible." "Only by being given opportunities to write can a student be taught how to write." "A good composition is not merely written. It is composed. So our teachers over a period of years have worked to cultivate and guide students' thought processes." "Grammar is learned through writing rather than by memorizing rules." "We have been making a deliberate attempt to concentrate on writing skills. In this attempt we have emphasized clear, concise, objective writing, often using discussion of problems arising in the literature assignments as theme topics."

C. Special attention to able students

"An accelerated or enriched program for high I.Q. students." "Awareness of school personnel concerning needs of above-average pupils." "Homogeneous grouping in English classes." "Our honors program, a four-year advanced course in which the class size ranges from 20 to 30." "Small classes for excellent students."

D. Strong program in reading and literature

"Concentration on good literature from seventh through twelfth grade." "A reading improvement program available to all students." "A summer reading program." "Students read widely." "A reading program which encourages use of library." "Variety of studies in diversified literature, with emphasis on further individual study." "Our advanced students are urged to undertake a more advanced program in reading."

E. Emphasis on fundamentals of English

"Formal grammar, correct usage, capitalization and punctuation stressed throughout the four years." "Though we teach much grammar, we do not let that substitute for writing." "Drill in the mechanics of good writing." "We have used the functional approach for teaching grammatical concepts." "Stress on writing mechanics. Much oral drill which requires reasoning and explanation is given along with extensive blackboard work. The dictionary is always consulted when questions of pronunciation, meaning, and derivation arise."

F. Superior homes and backgrounds of students

"Parental interest." "A home of culture." "The girl has not been culturally deprived." "A large number of cultivated homes where children absorb the humanities naturally." "Family reading backgrounds." "Homes in which learning is respected."

G. Carefully planned curriculum

"Sequence of work from level to level is carefully developed." "Cooperative and long-range planning." "Integration of the four areas of communication: listening, speaking, reading, and writing." "We have set up a course of study to ensure the teaching of all phases at one time or another and to eliminate unwarranted duplication." "Unified efforts to teach a progressive spiral course of skills and to inspire students to read widely with increased vocabulary and enthusiasm for knowledge of the past and the world around them." "A spirally developed four-year program set up to provide systematic growth."

H. Earlier preparation of students

"High quality of previous instruction." "A good English program from grades 1-12." "Solid foundation in junior high." "Good teachers from the first grade on."

I. School emphasis on academic achievement

"Our school is in a community which places heavy emphasis on academic achievement." "Tradition of high performance in English." "The demanding program has made intellectual achievement more 'fashionable' than athletic endeavor." "We honor our young writers in assembly programs." "Our school has an unbroken record of success in academic accomplishment of all kinds." "Encouraging literary as well as athletic excellence." "A general high standard of conduct and achievement set by the school system and community." "Achievement by brain gets equal recognition with achievement by brawn." "Attempt to live up to the slogan 'The School That Leads.'" "Fifty years of emphasis on intellectual challenge." "Since our students have shown no great athletic ability, the people have grown more education-minded than in many places."

J. Able administrators, interested in English

"High standards outlined by the principal." "A sympathetic administration." "An interested administration." "Able administrators." "Administrative emphasis on importance of academic work." "We have a free hand in choosing materials. I am using *1984, The Red Badge of Courage,* and *The Ox-Bow Incident* now in theme studies of utopia, fear, and justice, though two of these are sometimes considered borderline." "Strong support of language arts programs by district superintendent and other administrators, especially their concern for the composition program." "An administration highly interested in promoting academic achievement."

K. Possession and use of a good library

"Excellent school library." "Excellent cooperation with the librarians." "Our facilities are excellent: classrooms, library, and classroom libraries." "Good library with a fine cooperative librarian who works with the teachers in the library and the classroom."

L. Community interest in education

"Cultural and intellectual climate of the community." "Community interest in achievement of students." "Our community is highly literate." "Proximity of cultural offerings."

M. Reasonable teacher load

"Smaller classes than the average school." "Relatively small classes." "Classes below 25." "Our English teachers have four classes. Their schedule includes one period for conference and planning and one period of study hall supervision. Class enrollments between 25 and 30." "In 12th grade we have fourteen top students in a class." "Effort not to overload classes, thereby allowing more individual help per student."

N. School departmental insistence on high standards

"Standards high in English work." "Master teachers who insist that students work to their capacity." "High standards which school tries to maintain." "Tone of the school sets standard for achievement and encourages achievement in all academic areas." "Persistent pursuit of excellence."

O. **Availability of educational materials**

> "Plenty of resources for the classroom and in the library." "Plenty of films; multiple textbooks." "Excellent facilities and materials provided by a cooperative and sympathetic administration." "Good instructional materials, including textbooks, reference books, and audio-visual aids."

P. **Close cooperation of English teachers**

> "Departmental cooperation." "We have a department the members of which work together and are interested in their subject." "Good rapport among the teachers." "Agreement on objectives."

Q. **Vocabulary work**

> "Vocabulary stressed throughout the four years." "Sequential study of words in grades 7-12." "I am insistent on regular spelling and vocabulary drill."

R. **Others (fewer than 20 responses each)**

> "Frequent conferences with students" (mentioned 9 times). "Close liaison with colleges" (8). "Follow-up studies of students' performance in college" (3). "Cooperation of other departments" (17). "In-service training of teachers" (8). "Use of lay readers" (8). "Emphasis on teaching of thinking" (18). "Teachers who keep up to date with professional developments" (19).

15. DEPARTMENTAL NEEDS

What do you consider the crucial needs of your English department at the present time?

Comment: Even these schools which produce superior students feel that, given a fair chance, they could do better work. Again and again comes the cry for fewer classes and smaller classes, less for the sake of the teachers than for the good of the students; over a third of these responses echo that plea. The following answers, many of which were frequently repeated, typify other "crucial needs":

Materials and facilities

"Supplementary materials"
"Dictionaries, classroom libraries with paperback editions, reference books, books for enriching the curriculum"
"Better library facilities"
"Better library service"
"Larger classroom libraries"
"More audio-visual aids"
"Good films and recordings"

"We need a very large stock of books, magazines, and newspapers of the best kind, tape-recording equipment for self-analysis, and duplicating machines, overhead projectors, and other devices for keeping cumulative progress records and adapting lessons to our needs of the moment"
"More books in library"
"An adequate textbook supply"
"Elimination of workbooks"
"Special materials for advanced and retarded groups"
"More reference books in each classroom"
"Dictionaries in each classroom"
"Composition correcting machines!"
"More classroom space"
"A professional library for the use of English teachers"
"For each teacher, a room of her own, so that she may have her files, tools, boards, and classroom library available when needed"
"We have books, but no place to store them; we have students with no place to teach them; we have tests and equipment, but no central place to keep them; we are a department of fifteen teachers without an office. Our crying need is Space!"

Personnel

"Either lay readers or (preferably) more qualified teachers"
"Reduction of teacher turnover"
"Better trained teachers"
"Additional teachers to engage in remedial and developmental reading"
"Teachers who have had more hours of English"
"A supply of dynamic teachers"
"More dedicated teachers"
"More teachers with master's degrees in English"
"More supervision (by someone whose field is English) and in-service training"
"Coordinator of junior and senior high school English"
"A real appreciation on the part of the administration of the importance of English—not just lip service"
"Some secretarial help"
"A head of the department with time and ability to supervise the work"
"Teachers with more knowledge of current trends in English"
"Our department is staffed in part by housewives who teach as an avocation. We need more men teachers of English. We need experts, or at least those who aspire to be, not part time amateurs who merely like to think that they enjoy teaching English."

Curriculum and instruction

"More uniform planning throughout the department, and particularly a planned development in reading from grade 1 through grade 12"
"More work in writing and speaking"
"Increased emphasis on composition"
"Homogeneous grouping"
"More opportunity to help the 'slow' and 'bright' as individuals"
"More time on improving reading for comprehension"
"Correlation of English with other subjects (cooperation from other departments)"
"Time for student conferences"
"A sequential development of English teaching"

"More long range planning"
"An organized staff working toward common objectives"
"A course of study that incorporates some of the ideas involved in modern linguistics"
"Continuing study of standards"
"More time for better preparation of lessons and units"
"We should do more for the gifted students"
"A planning period for each teacher"
"More emphasis on spelling and vocabulary"
"Our most crucial need is to develop within our students some ideas more profound than those which they gather from their narrow teenage world. . . . Our graduates are able to write, but they don't have anything to say."

Summary

The samples of answers to question 15 show that these English departments have problems not unlike those in other schools. Even in these schools help is needed. The answers reveal also the dedication, the professional zeal, of the teachers in the departments from which the NCTE Achievement Award winners come, and the earnestness with which these teachers constantly seek to improve their instruction.

The respondents acknowledge, almost without exception, that their English programs are not perfect, that they do not know all the answers. Yet, if producing superior students is a mark of a superior department, these departments are superior.

The highlights at the beginning of this section summarize the most important findings of the questionnaire. It seems reasonable to assume that the nation's schools may produce still more superior English students when most of the English departments may be described with the same ten statements.

THE NEED FOR BETTER AND MORE BASIC RESEARCH IN ENGLISH

A strong national program of research to improve the teaching of English is essential to developing more efficient methods of teaching. Such a program needs both coordination and leadership. Ways must be found to support long range studies of language development, cooperative research projects, and other investigations which require resources greater than those most individuals possess. Special efforts are needed to interest qualified investigators in the crucial problems faced by teachers of English. Better methods must be found to disseminate information on research under way and on research completed.

The kinds of crucial questions about which teachers of English seek answers are many. During the spring of 1960, forty-one officers and committee chairmen of the National Council of Teachers of English were asked to identify important research needs in English. Their answers, partially reproduced below, indicate the kinds of research which are needed.

Studies in language are stressed in this list largely because the profession faces so many unresolved problems in this area. However, research in literature and the teaching of literature must also be supported and encouraged.

Some Needed Research in Language Development

1. Reinterpretation of language development of children in terms of present day structural linguistics.
    (a) A review and reinterpretation of the findings and methods of study in such existing classics as Piaget's *Language and Thought of the Child*, Gregoire's *L'Apprentissage du Language*, and Stern's *Die Kindersprache*.
    (b) Further investigations into areas where these studies have not penetrated, e.g.,
       —Inflectional features of English, particularly irregular verb forms
       —The emergence of the phonemic system in the child
       —The development of sentence patterns
2. A study of the emotional, psychological, physiological, experiential, and educational differences between good and poor writers at the high school level.
3. An investigation of the use of oral-aural approaches in teaching standard English to substandard speakers.

4. An analysis of the skills, knowledge, attitudes, and understandings included in various kinds of language proficiency and the standards of achievements which serve as the bases of evaluating competency in each area. A committee of the NCTE has suggested that at least six broad types of language proficiency may be identified: communicative, creative, interpretative, editorial, scholarly, technical. From such a study would come better instruments for measuring various kinds of proficiency.
5. An investigation of language attitudes at various socio-economic levels, including an analysis of regional differences.
6. The development and standardization of new tests of language achievement for students in various age groups.

Some Needed Research in Learning

1. Long range studies of concept development, including the analysis of how concepts are best introduced throughout the school program. Included would be a study of the relation of concept formation to language development and to social and psychological factors.
2. A comparison of the motivating power of new linguistic materials compared with traditional materials in developing language consciousness in students, e.g., the interest generated by concentration on the learner's own language, on his speech patterns, on his vocabulary. What are the effects of learning a foreign language on pupils' oral and written development in English in the elementary school? What is the effect of study of the communication process on the improvement of pupils' oral and written expression?

Some Needed Research in Methods of Teaching

1. An assessment of the uses of educational television in teaching, drawing together results from many small experimental programs announced during the past decade. An objective assessment of the uses of TV has yet to be made.
2. Comparative studies of the effectiveness of different kinds of instructional organization and new patterns of teaching language and literature, e.g.,
    (a) teaching machines and programmed learning
    (b) lay readers

(c) small composition classes under individual teachers versus large lecture sessions with assistants to conduct small recitation and conference groups
  (d) team teaching
3. An evaluation of ways of developing understanding and appreciation of literature at different developmental levels. Further investigations of such approaches as the following:
  (a) explication
  (b) historical survey
  (c) the core curriculum
  (d) the thematic or topical unit
  (e) the small seminar with stress on critical theory and critical analysis
  (f) intensive versus extensive reading
4. A study of the effect of compulsory reading programs in the junior high school on the attitudes, abilities, and learning of students.

Present funds available to support basic research in English are limited. The Cooperative Research Program of the U. S. Office of Education has been limited in scope and funds. Experimentation supported under Title VII of the National Defense Education Act of 1958 must concentrate on the uses of newer media of communication rather than on the teaching of subject matter through these media. More than one-half of the projects supported by this act are concerned not with the contrast of instruction but with methods and techniques in using communication media.[1] Large national foundations have been generous in supporting certain kinds of experimentation, such as school programming or the use of television, but too seldom is adequate provision made for evaluating results in many of these field programs. Also, the interest of foundations has necessarily been restricted to supporting certain kinds of projects. Unfortunately, the answer to many important basic questions facing teachers of English will not be found in experimentation now underway. What is needed is systematic and thorough support for projects in many different areas.

---

[1] Letter from C. H. Moore, Assistant to the Commission of Education, April 29, 1960.

A FINAL WORD

The teaching of English will become effective only as the conditions under which it is taught improve. Present programs for preparing English teachers must be reassessed and new programs developed to assist many practicing teachers. School libraries must be expanded; teaching loads, reduced. Research must supply better answers for some of the English teachers' urgent questions. A national reawakening of interest and activity in English is long overdue.

Our political democracy can provide our youth with the conditions of liberty—abundance, freedom of action, an accessible system of schools. But the ability to think and write and read, and an intimate contact with ideals, beauty, and morality—all central in English studies—are needed to equip our citizens to use their freedom wisely. America is now a major world power. As never before our country must think about its responsibilities to mankind and about its need for citizens to meet these awesome responsibilities. Tomorrow's leaders must learn today whatever truth and beauty and wisdom our culture can provide. Only a quality education will prepare our youth for the test; only a balanced education will assure the quality needed. National interest demands vigorous leadership to improve all educational programs.

INDEX

A

Abilities in language, 11
Achievement Awards program
    Analysis of schools, 116-132
    Procedures, 115
Allen, Harold B., 60, 62, 63
American Association of School Librarians, 101-102
American Bar Association, 18
American Council of Learned Societies, 7
American Federation of Teachers, 86
American Library Association, 121
American Mathematics Association, 12
Ann Arbor Conference, 1951, 29
Architecture
    For classrooms, 9-10
    For libraries, 9-10
Articulation in English teaching, 5-6, 27
Associated Research Councils, 29
Association of Graduate Schools, 18
Attitudes toward English, 17-18, 24, 27-28
Audio-visual aids, 10, 24, 134

B

Bloomfield, Leonard, 61, 74

C

Center for Applied Linguistics, 29
Certification standards for teachers
    College work required for general certification, 44-45
    Elementary certificate, 45
    English requirements, 45-46
    Minimum standards, 33
    Secondary certificate, 46-48
Class size, 11, 34, 90-91, 97-98, 99, 118, 135
College-high school team programs, 4, 5
College Entrance Examination Board
    Examinations, 23
    Commission on English, 70
Colleges
    Independent, 9
    Small, 7
    Teachers, 4, 6, 8, 9, 36-37

Committee on Preparation and Certification of Teachers, 39
Commission on the Curriculum, 70
Communication
    In democracy, 16
    Oral-aural, 24, 133
Composition for college freshmen, 36-37, 55, 70
Composition in the high school, 70, 91-93, 120
Conant, James B., 19, 70, 97
Conditions for teaching, 10-11, 89-100
Conference on College Composition and Communication, 62
Coordination between state and local school districts, 5, 87
Culturally depressed communities, 8-9
Curriculum material development, 5-6, 9

D

Distribution of information
    Careers for English specialists, 12
    Pilot programs, 6
    Teacher education, 6-7
Doctoral programs in teaching of English, 9
Dusel, William J., 92-95, 100
Duties of English teachers
    Extra-curricular, 26, 90, 95, 99
    Teaching of composition, 91-94, 99

E

Educational campaign throughout country, 4-5
Electronic aids, 10, 134
Elementary school methods course, 59
    Children's literature, 58
    Language arts, 57, 59
    Reading, 57, 58, 59
English as a foreign language, 29
English departments in high school
    Courses of study, 125
    Departmental needs, 130-132
    English requirements, 117-118
    Factors of success, 126-127

English methods course, 71, 84-85
    Structural linguistics, 73
    Teaching composition, 73
    Teaching English usage, 72
    Teaching literature, 85
    Teaching of formal grammar, 72
Enrollments
    In college, 22
    In elementary school, 19-22
    In high school, 19-22
Essentiality of English, 17-18, 29-30
Examinations for prospective teachers and supervisors, 4, 11

F

Financial assistance to teachers
    English and humanities students, 11, 37
    Loans, 7
    Scholarships, 7
Focus of English teaching, 26
Fries, Charles C., 75

G

General Education in a Free Society (Harvard), 92
Goals of improvement in English teaching, 3, 96-98, 114, 127-130
Grouping
    Heterogeneous, 5
    Homogeneous, 91
    Inter-age, 11

H

Highlights of chapters, 33, 43, 48, 60, 75, 89, 100, 104, 114
Hook, J. N., 114
Humanistic studies, 7, 8, 11, 15-16, 27, 28

I

In-service education, 4, 5, 8
Independent schools and colleges, 9
Internship programs, 11

K

Kowalski, Representative Frank, 7

L

Lancet, 18
Latimer, John F., 18
Lay readers, 11, 134
Leadership training, 5, 9
Libraries
    Architecture, 9-10
    Books, 10, 121
    Facilities, 10, 100-104, 121
    Standards, 101-102
Linguistic Society of America, 29, 61
Linguistic studies
    Applications to teaching, 8, 73, 74-75
    In English, 61
    NCTE statements on, 61-62
    Qualifications to teach, 36
    Structural linguistics for teachers, 73
    Surveys of, 62, 63
    Textbooks, 63
Literary heritage, 16, 17

M

Majors in English
    Education courses, 71, 84-85
    General literature preparation, 77-78
    Language preparation, 66, 69
    Minimum preparation, 46
    Practicing teachers, 36, 123
    Specific literature preparation, 78-84
Mersand, Joseph, 18, 27
Metropolitan School Study Council, 91
Minors in English (see Non-majors)
Modern Language Association, 29

N

National Association of Secondary-School Principals, 70
National Defense Education Act, 1958, 10, 11, 29, 135
National Education Association, 21, 86
National Humanities Foundation, 28
National institute program
    In articulation, 4, 5
    In language, literature, and composition, 4, 7
Non-major English teachers, 7-8, 35, 66, 71, 86

P

Personnel for teacher training, 6, 36
Pilot programs
    Experiments in teaching, 8
    National evaluation, 8
    Teacher education, 6
Preparation of practicing teachers, 7-9, 12, 74-75, 86, 134-135, 136
Preparation of elementary teachers, 48-60
    Elementary school methods, 57, 59
    English in addition to freshman English, 52-53, 55-57
    Freshman English, 51-52
    Language history and structure, 54-55
    Literature, 53-54
    Reading, 57, 59
    Specialized professional education, 58
    Subject major outside of education, 51
Preparation of secondary teachers, 60-86
    Language, 60-75
        Advanced composition, 70
        Availability of courses, 67-68
        Methods in composition, 73-74
        Minimal credit requirements, 66
        Structural linguistics, 73
    Literature, 75-86
        Deficiencies in requirements, 86
        Genre courses, 82-83
        Methods in literature, 85
        Minimal credit requirements, 77-78
        Specific courses, 78-80
Preparation of teachers, general, 6-7, 21-23, 134-135
Prevalence of English instruction, 18-19

Q

Quality of education, 9, 28, 38, 136

R

Recruitment of teachers, 11-12, 36
Regional study centers
    Demonstration of sequential programs, 5-6
    For consultant help for teachers, 9
    For graduates of small colleges, 7
    For preparation of teaching aids, 9

Remedial English
    Cost, 104, 111-112
    Credit granted, 112-113
    Faculty assignments, 110-111
    In college, 23, 104-114
    In general, 23
    Offerings, 109
Requisites for teaching English, 40
Research and scholarship
    Basic problems, 10, 11
    Class size, 11, 90-91
    Needs
        Language development, 133-134
        Learning, 134
        Methods of teaching, 134-135
    Projects for, 10-11
    Teaching conditions, 11, 89
    Utilization of time, 11
Rice, Warner G., 37
Rockefeller Report, 1959, 20, 22, 36

S

Salaries of teachers, 86
School population
    Changing nature of, 9
    Heterogeneity, 5
    Increase, 21-23
Seminars during school year, 4, 7, 8
Slaughter, Eugene E., 39, 44
Social value of English, 16-17
Standard of preparation to teach English
    Abilities, 41-42
    Knowledge, 41
State departments of education
    Coordination with local districts, 5, 87
    English specialists, 5
    State superintendents, 6
Study of language, literature, and composition, 4-5, 60-87, 117, 122, 124-125
Substandard education, 26, 33, 34
Summaries of chapters, 48, 60, 74, 86, 113, 132
Summer institutes
    For academically talented high school students, 12
    For college instructors, 8
    For graduates of small colleges, 7
    For non-majors, 7-8
    For self-education in the humanities, 7
    To apply new knowledge of teaching, 4

Supply of teachers
    College, 36-37
    Elementary, 21, 33-34, 50
    General, 23, 33-38
    Secondary, 19, 21, 34-36, 65
Syntax, 75

T

Teacher-load
    Class size, 90-91
    NCTE resolutions, 96, 119
    Reduction, 28
    Summaries of facts, 98-100
    Work-week, 94-95
Team teaching, 11, 135
Testing of language competence (in college)
    Cost of testing program, 107-108
    Number of institutions testing, 105
    Number of students tested, 105
    Percentage of failures, 106-107
Textbooks
    Linguistics, 63
    Quality of, 104
    Selection, 11

U

United States Office of Education, 6, 11, 12, 22, 135

V

Visiting Scholar Program, 12

W

Ward, Barbara, 29
Warner, J. C., 18
Watson, W. W., 18
White House Conference on Children and Youth, 1960, 16, 28, 104
Wyld, Henry Cecil, 61

Y

Yarborough, Senator Ralph, 7

Notes

Notes